African-American Studies
Core List of Resources

An Annotated List of Selected Resources
Used by Teachers of African-American Studies
at Colleges and Universities in the United States
During the 1998-99 Academic Year

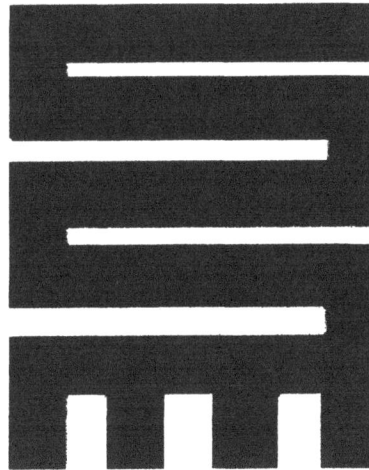

African-American Studies
Core List of Resources

An Annotated List of Selected Resources
Used by Teachers of African-American Studies
at Colleges and Universities in the United States
During the 1998-99 Academic Year

Compiled by

Akilah Shukura Nosakhere
Robert W. Woodruff Library, Atlanta University Center

M. Elaine Hughes
Georgia State University Library

Anne Page Mosby
Mercer University Swilley Library

African-American Studies Core List of Resources

ISBN-10: 1-932846-01-8
ISBN-13: 978-1-932846-01-0

Library of Congress Control Number: 2004109342

THE BLACKBURN PRESS
P. O. Box 287
Caldwell, New Jersey   07006   U.S.A.
973-228-7077
www.BlackburnPress.com

DEDICATION

This work is dedicated to those courageous African-American students, known and unknown, who risked their academic careers and their very lives to demand that their history be taught in institutions of higher education across America.

PREFACE

The African-American Studies Core List of Resources (Core List) is the product of a grant from Whitney-Carnegie awarded initially to four Georgia State University librarians by the American Library Association Publishing Committee in October 1997. The initial team members were: M. Elaine Hughes, Anne Page Mosby, and Akilah Nosakhere, Project Manager, and Kimberly Parker, a Ph.D. candidate in Library and Information studies at Florida State University. Dr. Parker was instrumental in developing the survey forms. In 1999, Dr. Parker returned to Tallahassee to complete her doctoral studies.

The African-American Studies Core List includes a number of classic works by early African-American studies scholars that may be out of print but are not necessarily unavailable to the serious seeker. Local research collections housed at the Auburn Avenue Research Library on African-American Culture and History, Georgia State University Library, Emory University's Robert W. Woodruff Library, and the Robert W. Woodruff Library Special Collections of the Atlanta University Center were all instrumental in the completion of records for this project.

I am very proud to note that the majority of the books abstracted for the Core List were available from research collections within the city of Atlanta. In particular, I found the John Henrik Clarke Africana Collection at "AUC Woodruff" to be a godsend. Some of the rare titles were found in this collection just a few feet away from my desk. Thank you, Ancestor.

We are indebted to retired Pullen Library administrators, Dr. Ralph Russell (*Mr. GALILEO*) and Dr. Carolyn Robison, for their belief in the Core List project and their confidence in our ability to juggle our library responsibilities to carry out this important work. Special thanks to Dr. Charles Jones, chairman of the African-American Studies Department at Georgia State University, for encouraging us not to give up on the project. We are appreciative of the support provided by Dr. Jacqueline Wade, Past President of the National Council for Black Studies, and the membership who participated in the 1999 survey.

Over the years, we have had several student assistants to work on this project. We thank them all: Kimberly Parker (research partner and Florida State University graduate student), Fanny Garvey, Starr Johnson, Babatunde Nasiru, and Shawn Trotter, all of Georgia State University; and Brian Shields of the Interdenominational Theological Center. Our students helped search and harvest on-line catalogs to complete citations for each title in the database. In addition, they retrieved titles from the stacks and initiated dozens of Inter Library Loan forms so that we could write abstracts from the real thing. We take full responsibility for any errors or omissions and for all of its shortcomings.

Akilah S. Nosakhere
M. Elaine Hughes
Anne Page Mosby
Atlanta, Georgia
May 2004

CONTENTS

INTRODUCTION

Traditionally, the discipline of African-American studies has focused primarily on the history of black people in the United States. However, African-American studies also include the study of African people and their influences in Canada, Mexico, Central and South America, as well as the Caribbean Islands and Cuba. Moreover, scholarly resources on the study of the African experience in America are available not only in English but also in the Spanish, French, and Portuguese languages, among others. The breadth and depth of African-American studies is much too vast to be captured in any one bibliographic endeavor. Therefore, this bibliographic work is limited to English-language titles appearing on five or more reading lists or syllabi of African-American studies faculty who responded to a national survey conducted in 1998 by three academic librarians at Georgia State University Library in Atlanta.

The continuation of African-American studies bibliography is essential if the discipline is to occupy a prominent place in higher education. As the body of scholarship in African-American studies continues to develop, Africana studies librarians are challenged to maintain management of these resources and create access that is convenient.

The African-American Studies Core List is an annotated checklist for use by academic librarians selecting materials for instruction and research in the field of African-American studies. Titles appearing on five or more faculty lists were collected in a *ProCite* database where complete bibliographic data, Library of Congress subject headings, call numbers, and abstracts were added to each title entry.

This African-American Studies Core List is made up of 304 key titles in 50 subject areas. It is a work focused exclusively on those common resources cited by teachers of African-American studies courses in U.S. colleges and universities. It is an annotated list of scholarly books, providing a "snapshot" of the resources used in the instruction of the "Black experience in the Americas" during a given academic year. Academic department administrators, researchers, publishers of Africana materials as well as librarians will find the Core List a useful instrument in the study of African-American bibliography.

I. POPULATION

The subjects were identified from the *Directory of Universities and Colleges with Programs in Africana Studies Within the United States of America, 1994-1995.*[1] The National Council for Black Studies (NCBS) published the directory listing those professors who were affiliated with African-American studies departments and programs at the university level within the United States.

The NCBS Directory listed 336 African-American studies (AAS) departments/programs and 1,532 faculty members who taught African-American studies in the United States. In January 1998, survey forms were mailed to all AAS departments and AAS teaching faculty identified in the Directory. By mid-March, 146 completed department survey questionnaires and 124 faculty/participant surveys were received.

II. METHODOLOGY AND PROCEDURE

Two slightly different survey forms were created to gather a variety of information from AAS teaching faculty. The survey forms were tested for validity with the departments of African-American Studies at Georgia State University in Atlanta and the University of Cincinnati.

The department survey was designed to collect data about the administrative structure of the African-American studies unit. We wanted to know if the unit was a true "department" or something else. The department questionnaire consisted of six questions requesting basic information regarding the type of institution, the start date

---

[1] National Council for Black Studies. *Directory of Universities and Colleges with Programs in Africana Studies within the United States of America, 1994-1995.* Carson, CA: National Council for Black Studies, 1994.

for teaching African-American studies at the institution, the number of courses offered, the most popular course, and the percentage of cross-listed courses. The department survey form was sent to department chairs or unit heads to complete (see Appendix A-Department Survey).

The participant survey was used to collect data on books and other materials used for class instruction and research activities. Instead of recording their reading lists onto the survey form, many respondents simply attached their course syllabi and reading lists. These attachments proved very useful in discovering frequently recommended titles and course offerings used in the construction of a collection development tool.

In addition, the participant survey forms collected information about the faculty educational level, years teaching, research interests, library habits, popular courses, and any subject areas where it is sometimes difficult to acquire research or instructional materials (see Appendix B-Participant Survey). By the end of March 1999, 122 completed questionnaires were returned. The survey return rate was about 11%. In spite of an average return rate, a count of books appearing on two or more faculty lists resulted in a title collection of over 1200 records. Given our time limitation, the annotation of 1200+ titles was not our objective so we changed our criteria and selected for annotation-only those books appearing on 5 or more course syllabi and recommended reading lists supplied by the faculty. To balance the number of subjects, we also deleted approximately 46 literary works to bring the bibliography closer to our goal of 300 titles. It is our belief that the interdisciplinary nature of African-American literature allows it to be easily captured in literary bibliographies, where as other more specialized titles may not be so easily integrated in other bibliographies. So, using this simplistic criterion, we were able to reduce the Core List to a manageable file of 304 titles.

III. LITERATURE SEARCH AND DISCUSSION

The arrival of black studies programs to state universities and colleges in 1969 prompted campus libraries to collect materials to support this "new" field of study. Around this same time many university libraries were experimenting with automatic acquisition methods, such as standing order and approval book plans with publishers and book vendors. Generally, mainstream publishers who managed these book plans had not yet recognized the marketability of African-American studies materials; therefore, few black titles were handled through these approval book plans.

From the onset of the 20th century, African-American studies scholars have found it difficult to publish their work with mainstream publishers. In spite of publisher rejections, African-American scholars found ways to publish and distribute their research. It was not unusual for African-American studies professors and librarians to create and publish their own teaching materials. For years, professors and librarians at historic black colleges and universities used their own funds to publish their research and often distributed their materials through their students, through study groups, at conferences, on the street, and through the mail. Examples of African-American studies pioneers include historians, bibliographers and librarians, such as Dr. W.E.B. Du Bois, Dr. Monroe Nathan Work, Dr. Carter G. Woodson, Dr. Charles Wesley, Laura Eliza Wilkes, Helen Adele Whiting, J.A. Rogers, Dr. Leo Hansberry, Dr. John G. Jackson, Dr. Chancellor Williams, Dr. John Henrik Clarke, Dr. Yosef Ben-Jochanan, Dr. Lenwood G. Davis, Dr. Darlene Clark Hine, Dr. Maulana Karenga, and librarians Delores C. Leffall and Dorothy Porter Wesley, to name a few.

In the 1960s and '70s, many black studies historians relied upon black publishers, small independent presses and university presses to produce small runs of their books. The market for these materials included mostly libraries of historically black colleges and universities and those of wealthy state and private institutions, like UCLA, UC Berkeley, San Francisco State University and Cornell University. Visionary collection development librarians and archivists at these institutions were the major collectors of these early materials, and today these libraries possess a broad selection of first editions of African-American studies texts as found in selected title analysis conducted in the Online Computer Library Center (OCLC) World Catalog.

In the 1980s, mainstream academic publishers began to offer general "Black Americana" encyclopedias, biographical and literary works about black people in America. The availability of these general works from specialized directories, encyclopedias, and literary collections on African America, in print and nonprint formats had become available for purchase by academic libraries and the individual researcher.

Today, African-Americana studies materials have achieved a place in mainstream publishing. The industry has come to recognize the value of this market and realize the important role of African-American studies in the provision of a "well-rounded" liberal arts education offered by U.S. institutions.

The bibliography is a traditional and standard tool used in libraries, museums and archives to review, manage and locate materials. An annotated bibliography is clearly useful because it is more than a title list—it is an analytical tool that assists in the search for little known facts or historical references. Annotated bibliographies enable librarians to locate key materials and to fill subject gaps or to strengthen certain subject areas in the collection.

Annotated bibliographies do not expire with time: they become more valuable as a "resource of resources" with tracings for possible future acquisition. Bibliographies also contain historic, significant, or unique information that makes them value to each generation of scholars. Occasionally in the collection decision-making process, it is wise to consult bibliographies for clarification or to find new research leads. For example, consulting an historic subject bibliography to find information about a title can help a subject specialist to decide whether to purchase an older edition of an African-American studies title as a replacement copy in the main stacks or alert the archivist or special collection librarian about a possible addition to the rare book collection.

For the African-American studies specialist, the use of print-based reviews, checklists, and bibliographies continues to be vital. While it is true the interdisciplinary nature of African-American studies permits the use of some general subject indexes and bibliographies for the collection of some relevant titles, specialized bibliographies are best because they tend to more detailed and thorough in content analysis.

An early example of an African-American studies bibliography is a small booklet entitled, "*The Negro in Print.*" A five-year compilation by librarian Dolores C. Leffall, this resource is a subject index of books, reports, journal articles and documents related to African-American life and culture covering the period of 1965-1970.

The Negro Bibliography and Research Center of Washington, DC, commissioned this bibliographical series in the late 1960s in celebration of "Negro History Week" in the nation's capital. The editor, Dolores C. Leffall, was school librarian at Anacostia High School. Out of print since 1972, this bibliography represents one of the first selection tools for Africana studies produced by a librarian; and it is still found in reference collections across the country today. The rich content of this bibliography include all types of materials on the black experience in America from 1966 through 1972. [2]

Throughout the 1970s and the early 1980s, only a few public and private academic libraries systematically collected curriculum materials in African-American studies. The reluctance of higher education to accept "black studies" as a bona fide discipline affected the library collection of early black studies materials outside of wealthy schools and historically black colleges and universities.

Fortunately, the 1990s has brought with it a renewal of interest in African-American studies on the college campus and a marked growth in the availability of Africana studies materials in the academic book market. Nearly every mainstream publisher has individual titles and/or series of titles dedicated to "black America." As a result, more and more traditional publishing companies, such as Gale, Bowker, Greenwood, Scarecrow, ProQuest (formerly UMI), G.K. Hall and even Time-Life Books, have produced general reference and some specialized resources to appeal to libraries collecting African-American studies material.

A review of the literature illustrates that today there are thousands of bibliographies on Africana studies in print. The subject matter exhibits great variety for every known interest. For instance, bibliographies range from a listing of titles to interest African-American youth, to specialized lists such as the bibliography authored by Sharyn Thompson in 1997, Historic African-American and African Caribbean Cemeteries, which may be of great interest to genealogists and scholars of Caribbean studies.

The bibliography continues to be very important tool in collection development and promotion. Museum directors and archivists use bibliographies to promote collections among scholars or the subject specialist, whereas

---

[2] Leffall, Dolores C., *Bibliographic Survey: the Negro in Print, Five Year Subject Index, 1965-1970,* Washington, DC: Negro Bibliographic and Research Center, 1971.

The bibliography continues to be very important tool in collection development and promotion. Museum directors and archivists use bibliographies to promote collections among scholars or the subject specialist, whereas the social worker may select a bibliography to provide a parent with a list of resources related to child rearing or communicating with teenage children. The use of such a specialized, yet basic, tool is endless.

Dr. Lenwood G. Davis of Winston-Salem State University in North Carolina has compiled nearly eighty bibliographies on numerous subjects in the field of African-American studies. His prolific offerings are comparable to that of Monroe N. Work, the Tuskegee editor of the 1928 classic bibliography, *The Bibliography of the Negro in Africa and America*.[3] Librarians, archivists and scholars alike routinely use Davis's bibliographies to locate unique resources and to fill existing gaps in university collections. Dr. Davis's bibliographies aid the subject specialist in the discovery of neglected and rare resources in African-American studies.

Dr. Asa Hilliard, a professor of African-American studies at San Francisco State University for 18 years and currently the Fuller E. Callaway Professor of Urban Education at Georgia State University, produced a bibliography of fifty core titles he considers to be essential references on the history of African people. When compared to this resource, the Core List contains many of the same scholars and titles. Scholars such as W.E.B. Du Bois, Edward W. Blyden, George Reid Andrews, Molefi Asante, Wa Thiong'o Ngugi and Ivan Van Sertima are well represented in the African-American Studies Core List of Resources.[4] Works by these prominent authors have become standard texts and are still read in African-American studies courses today.

Moreover, 40% of the black scholars with ten or more citations in the 2002 *ISI Arts and Humanities and Social Science Indexes* are represented in the Core List. This indicates that key resources were indeed identified in the 1999 survey, and these resources continue to be relevant and important works five years later.[5]

In addition to book and journal-based bibliographies, there are an increasing number of web-based bibliographies for African-American studies librarians and scholars to explore in cyberspace. Nationwide Africana studies and social science librarians at academic institutions have created portals to many AAS resources for use by faculty, students, and researchers worldwide. Some of these include Columbia, Rutgers, the University of Pennsylvania, Louisiana State, Iowa State, Arizona State, Berkeley, Cornell, Stanford, Yale, the University of South Alabama, Colby College, and many others. The African-American Studies Librarian section (AFAS) of the American Library Association are developing yet another bibliography with plans to add both historical as well as current resources.[6]

The African-American Studies Core List Project is a distinctive tool for the development of African-American studies collections designed to support the instruction and research efforts of faculty and students of African-American studies departments. The uniqueness of the Core List bibliography is that it is compiled exclusively from the syllabi and recommended reading lists of AAS instructors who participated in the initial survey. This Core List offers academic librarians a reputable tool for African-American studies collection development for years to come.

---

[3] Work, Monroe N. *Bibliography of the Negro in Africa and America.* New York: H.W. Wilson, 1928.

[4] Hilliard, Asa G. III. *Fifty-Plus Essential References on the History of African People.* Baltimore, MD: Black Classic Press, 1993.

[5] Editor. "JBHE's Citation Rankings of Black Scholars in the Social Sciences and the Humanities," *Journal of Blacks in Higher Education.* 39 (Spring 2003) pp.8, 10.

[6] African American Studies Librarians Section (AFAS) Association of College and Research Libraries American Library Association. "AFAS Core Books." 29 July 2004. 12 August 2004. <http://www.ala.org/ala/acrl/aboutacrl/acrlsections/africanam/corebooks.htm>.

IV. SURVEY RESULTS

Survey forms were mailed nationwide to 336 African-American studies departments and 1,521 faculty identified as instructors of African-American studies as reported in the 1995 directory of Africana programs published by the *National Council for Black Studies*. Approximately, one-third of the private and public institutions (112) completed and returned surveys. Over 124 AAS faculty members returned completed questionnaires. Instead of listing their textbooks on the survey form, many of them attached the syllabi reading list. By the end of the summer, we had collected and entered 1,233 book titles into the *ProCite* database and hired two student assistants to begin adding basic bibliographic data to the records.

An examination of the data revealed that 75 out of the 112 (84%) teach African-American studies classes at public institutions that grant degrees in African-American studies. Thirty-seven faculty members from private institutions participated in the survey, representing 41% of the total faculty respondents. Of these private schools, 16 reported that they did not grant African-American studies degrees of any kind.

Seventy-one (88%) of the 124 AAS faculty reported that the structure of the African-American studies curriculum in their institutions is that of an interdisciplinary program with many courses cross-listed in other departments. Forty-one or 31% of the respondents indicated that on their campus African-American studies is structured as a full department. The remaining 12 were defined as "centers" or "coordinating units." Surprisingly, only 10% of the institutions surveyed granted graduate level degrees in African-American studies.

It was discovered that the majority of respondents reported to have been teaching African-American studies for 10 to 20 years. Forty percent had taught African-American studies for 20 years or more, with the many of these respondents reporting to be tenured or on the tenure track (see Appendix C-Years of Teaching). Eighty-four percent of the 110 respondents were found to have the terminal Ph.D. degree in the field in which they taught.

The majority of AAS faculty with Ph.D. degrees in the social sciences and humanities, however, 14% reported having earned their terminal degree in Africana studies. A total of seven respondents held terminal degrees in the fields of education, jurisprudence and medicine. Less than ten respondents had only the bachelor's or master's degrees. These instructors were teachers of English, music, theatre, the visual and performing arts (see Appendix D-Educational Background of AAS Faculty).

Forty of 44 respondents reported that their administrative home was in discipline: African-American studies, 20; Africana studies, 15; black studies and ethnic studies, 2 each; and one faculty member reported his/her administrative home to be within the department of Pan-African studies. The responses reveal a variety of concentration within the discipline as reflected in the names of the department and courses offered. However, the top three departments in which AAS faculty are most likely to be found are the African-American studies, Africana studies or English departments (see Appendix E-Top Three Administrative Homes).

One hundred and eleven respondents described the size of their most recent African-American studies class, with the average class size among the respondents being about 55 students, while the smallest class was a graduate seminar of one. (This respondent explained that often graduate seminars open had only one student.) The largest class reported was an entry-level introduction to an African-American studies course of 555 students (see Appendix G-African-American Studies Class Size).

Fifty-eight percent of the faculty surveyed reported that they did not have any difficulty finding materials to support instruction or research in their libraries or campus bookstores. Of the 15% who did experience some difficulty finding print material, the reasons given were that libraries were slow to order materials and that items were often found to be out of print, damaged or missing from the stacks (see Appendix H-Difficulty Finding Materials). Approximately, 67% of the respondents reported that their library had the majority of items needed for instruction and research (see Appendix H-Difficulty Finding Materials). Well over half of the faculty surveyed affirmed that the library collections at their respective institutions were adequate and own those materials needed for instruction and research. Only 23% reported that the library sometimes did not have the materials they needed; often these items were articles from journals not subscribed to by the library.

The respondents reporting inadequate library journal holdings also reported that they were more likely to create special course packets or place their own material on library reserve when items were available from the university library. Other respondents cited that materials were unavailable due to a variety of reasons, such as the typical "lost, damaged and cannot be replaced," to the disturbing "very little funding for books in this area" (see Appendix I-Survey Responses).

V. CONCLUSION

Out of a database of 1,254 book titles, an annotated listing of 304 resources was created to serve as a bibliographic tool for collection development in African-American studies. This Core List is organized alphabetically by 50 Library of Congress (LOC) subject headings and includes LOC numbers, ISBN or LOC catalog numbers, and abstracts of various lengths. African and African-American literature made up a large portion of the titles collected. As a result, the number of literary works abstracted was limited and subdivided by location and gender. Many subject divisions are used in the Core List because of the highly interdisciplinary nature of African-American studies.

The format is styled after that used by Dr. Lenwood G. Davis in his 1985 bibliography entitled, "*A Bibliographical Guide to Black Studies Programs in the United States: An Annotated Bibliography*." While Dr. Davis's work includes journal articles and unpublished dissertations, the Core List concentrates on book resources with the belief that these books may become prime candidates for digitization at a later date. We predict that many of the authors and titles identified by this Core List will ultimately become available in some digital format as new Africana studies resources are developed and marketed. Some titles are currently available through digital book collection, such as *NetLibrary*, and web-based sites featuring historical books in the public domain.

Abstracts for the African-American Studies Core List were written from actual books found in academic libraries in the Atlanta metropolitan area. On occasion when a title is unavailable from the Atlanta-area libraries (GSU Pullen Library, AUC Woodruff, Emory Woodruff Libraries, or the Auburn Avenue Research Library on Black History and Culture), they were borrowed from regional universities via Inter-Library Loan (ILL) services. While the University of Georgia Library supplied a number of rare titles, it is important to note that the Dr. John Henrik Clarke Africana Collection housed at the Robert W. Woodruff Library, Atlanta University Center, proved to be a major source of rare academic titles noted by faculty in the nationwide survey.

Increasingly, African-American core lists are available in digital form; however, they tend to be limited to contemporary resources. Traditional print bibliographies are best used for the discovery of classic and little known works. Bibliographies in both formats are valuable tools for systematic development of Africana collections; therefore, it is advisable to utilize both formats for comprehensive collection development.

The African-American Studies Core List produced by this five-year study can assist librarians in identifying prominent scholars and educators in the field, as well as classic works about African-American life and culture. This Core List aids in the rediscovery of significant titles such as *A History of an African People* by Robert W. July, *The Slave Community* by John W. Blassingame and Rayford Logan's *Betrayal of the Negro: From Rutherford B. Hayes to Woodrow Wilson*.

Historic and well-cited studies conducted with African-American families by respected social scientists populate the Core List. Early works by Robert Hill and Robert Staples are included, as well as later studies by Harriette Pipes McAdoo and Drs. Nathan and Julia Hare. The scholarship represented in this Core List contributes to the solidity of African-American studies as an important and legitimate field of study and research in American institutions of higher education. Since the birth of African-American studies in the Academy some thirty-plus years ago, the discipline continues to develop and produce an impressive body of scholarly knowledge that is to be managed by librarians and made continuously accessible to each new generation of learners using traditional and contemporary tools.

SELECTED BIBLIOGRAPHY

Aldridge, Dolores P. and Young, Carlene. *Out of the Revolution: The Development of Africana Studies*. New York, NY: Lexington Books, 2000.

Asante, Molefi Kete. "African-American Studies: The Future of the Discipline." *The Black Scholar*. 22, No.3 (1992): 20-28.

Conyers, James L., Jr. *Africana Studies: A Disciplinary Quest for Both Theory and Method*. Jefferson, NC: McFarland and Company, 1997.

Davis, Lenwood, G. and Hill, George. *A Bibliographical Guide to Black Studies Programs in the United States: An Annotated Bibliography*. Westport, CT: Greenwood Press, 1985.

Gates, Henry Louis. "African-American Studies in the 21st Century Publication." *The Black Scholar*. 22:3 (Summer 1992).

Hall, Raymond L. *Black Separatism and Social Reality: Rhetoric and Reason*. New York, NY: Pergamon Press, Inc., 1977.

Hall, Perry A. *In the Vineyard: Working in African-American Studies*. Knoxville, TN: University of Tennessee, 1999.

Hilliard, Asa G. III. *Fifty-Plus Essential References on the History of African People*. Baltimore, MD: Black Classic Press, 1993.

Editor, "JBHE's Citation Rankings of Black Scholars in the Social Sciences and the Humanities." *The Journal of Blacks in Higher Education*. No. 39, (2003): 8-10.

Karenga, Maulana. *Introduction to Black Studies*. Los Angeles, CA: University of Sankore Press, 1989.

Leffall, Dolores C., *Bibliographic Survey: The Negro in Print, Five-Year Subject Index, 1965-1970*. Washington, DC: Negro Bibliographic and Research Center, 1971.

National Council for Black Studies. *Directory of Universities and Colleges with Programs in Africana Studies within the United States of America, 1994-1995*. Carson, CA: National Council for Black Studies, 1995.

Thompson, Sharyn. *Historic African-American and African Caribbean Cemeteries: A Selected Bibliography*. Tallahassee, FL: The Center for Historic Cemeteries Preservation, 1997.

Thorpe, Earl E. *Negro Historians in the United States*. Baton Rouge, LA: Fraternal Press, 1958.

CORE LIST OF RESOURCES

ANTHROPOLOGY-AFRICA

1. Diop, Cheikh Anta. **The Cultural Unity of Black Africa: The Domains of Patriarchy and of Matriarchy in Classical Antiquity**. Chicago, IL: Third World Press, 1978.

    Diop is the first Francophone African scholar to use the Afrocentric approach to history to *"furnish the African sociological actuality."* This work is one of three books representing his investigation into African history and culture written for his Doctorate of Letters. Though based on sound scientific methods of discovery and documentation, white scholars *"started a rage against him that has not abated"* and much of his work is difficult to find. In this work, the author looks into the role of patriarchy in Europe, Africa, Australia and other parts of the world. Diop reveals that most of the world practices matriarchy. In Africa, he writes, both social systems have *"peacefully emerged."* This edition includes a new introduction by John Henrik Clarke.

    GN480.4 D513 1978
    0883780496

2. Kenyatta, Jomo. **Facing Mount Kenya: The Tribal Life of the Gikuyu**. New York, NY: Vintage Books, 1968.

    This is a first-hand account of the Gikuyu culture by a Gikuyu scholar educated in England. The work is praised as an *"unusual extent the knowledge of Western ways and Western modes of thought with a training and outlook essentially African."* The author is more widely known as an African Nationalist and first president of the independent Kenya. Jomo Kenyatta produced this study for a degree in Anthropology from the London School of Economics. It is described as an invaluable document in the area of culture contact and change.

    DT433 .545 K55 K46
    LC64-11495

3. Zaslavsky, Claudia. **Africa Counts: Number and Pattern in African Culture**. Chicago, IL: Lawrence Hill & Company, 1999.

    This work is a scholarly examination of the mathematical methods of selected African cultures beginning with mathematical traditions of ancient Egypt as noted in the Rhind Papyrus of 1650 B.C. to *"socio-mathematics"* of Africa as noted in modern African cultures. The author also examines the applications of mathematics in the everyday lives of African people and the influence African institutions have upon the evolution of mathematics in African cultures. The book is organized into eight sections and twenty-five chapters and includes illustrations, tables, charts, an appendix with extensive chapter notes and biographical notes on Schmidl and other important resources. This work includes an introduction by John Henrik Clarke. The most useful resources were German and French works not yet available in English. A German study entitled: *Zahl Und Zahlen in Afrika* by Marianne Schmidl is cited as the most helpful in this novel work.

    GN476.1 Z37
    1556523505

ANTHROPOLOGY-UNITED STATES

1. Bradley, Michael. **Iceman Inheritance: Prehistoric Sources of Western Man's Racism, Sexism and Aggression**. New York, NY: Warner Books, 1981.

    The author contends "*Europeans have an inferiority complex about their world position and therefore attempt to control the world through racism.*" The author writes that Europe appeared on the world scene much later than civilizations of the Nile Valley and other river valleys in Africa, Western Asia (the Middle East), Asia and Japan. He adds that Europe has historically used racist policies and practices to advance western culture throughout the world. The author points to the "*bastardization of Egypt*" by Alexander the Great and the establishment of the Trans-Atlantic slave trade which ignited Europe's economic recovery in the fifteenth and sixteenth centuries as examples of racist practices resulting from the inferiority complex suffered by "*Caucasians.*" The author offers theories related to cold environment, genetics, and culture to explain European aggression and preoccupation with death and destruction through technological means.

    GN537 .B7
    0446935069

BLACK MUSLIM MOVEMENT

1. Breitman, George. **Malcolm X Speaks: Selected Speeches and Statements**. New York, NY: Pathfinder, 1989.

    This work is a collection of nine speeches made by Malcolm X delivered during his last year of life. The purpose of this work is to provide a record of Malcolm's own ideas "*expounded and defended during his last year.*" The collection includes two speeches delivered in Harlem to McComb, Mississippi youth in Harlem and at the headquarters of the Freedom Democratic Party (FDP) in Harlem in support of Fannie Lou Hamer as the FDP candidate for Congress in 1964. Malcolm's letters from abroad are included with illustrations and an index.

    BP223 Z8 L5795
    0873485467

2. Clarke, John Henrik. **Malcolm X: The Man and His Times**. New York, NY: Macmillan, 1978.

    This book examines the life and meaning of Malcolm X in six parts. Part one reveals the effect of Malcolm X upon a generation of blacks in America as revealed in essays by Rev. Albert Cleage, Wyatt Tee Walker, C. Eric Lincoln and others. Part two provides a look at Malcolm X from the personal perspectives of associates and friends such as Shirley Graham Du Bois, Ossie Davis, and his wife, Betty Shabbazz. Part three is a collection of dialogue with Malcolm X. This section includes an essay by Mburumba Kerina entitled, "An African's View of Malcolm X," as well as Gordon Parks' last meeting with Malcolm, text from TV interviews, text from a secretly taped visit from the FBI to Malcolm's home and from a telephone conversation with Cuban nationalist Carlos Moore. Part four, entitled "Malcolm X Abroad," contains firsthand accounts of Malcolm's visits to Europe and Africa by historian Essiem-Udom, Lebert Bethune, Leslie A. Lacy and others. Part five features "Malcolm in his Own Words" and contains speeches delivered in the United States, Africa and Europe. The appendix includes seven speeches delivered between 1963-1964, including Malcolm's speech to the OAU (Organization of African Unity) in 1964, the statement of basic aims and objectives of the OAAU (Organization of African-American Unity), and the outline for the Petition to the UN charging genocide Against 22 million black Americans, and the eulogy delivered by Ossie Davis at the Faith Temple Church of God in New York.

    E185.97 L75 C55
    LC77-75902

3. Epps, Archie. **The Speeches of Malcolm X at Harvard**. New York, NY: Morrow, 1968.
   This work is a collection of speeches made by Malcolm X at Harvard University in March and December of 1964. They appear with the comments made by the author regarding the psychological makeup of Malcolm X and the "*most romantic*" of his speeches at Harvard. It includes full text of the speeches, personal and societal circumstances in which Malcolm X spoke, and an interesting analysis of Malcolm X as an angry man and his political activity as "*a side product of a strategy of escape.*"
   > E185.61 L59 1968
   > LC68-19425

4. Haley, Alex. **Autobiography of Malcolm X**. New York, NY: Grove Press, 1965.
   This book details the life of Malcolm X a.k.a El-Hajj Malik El-Shabazz as told to and recorded by Alex Haley. M.S. Handler writes the introduction, the epilogue is by Alex Haley, and there is a final segment by Ossie Davis on why he eulogized Malcolm. The 1992 edition published by Ballantine Books contains a foreword by Attallah Shabazz, the eldest daughter of El-Hajj Malik El-Shabbazz and Betty Shabazz.
   > E185.97 L5 A3
   > 0394171225

5. Lomax, Louis E. **When the Word is Given: A Report of Elijah Muhammad, Malcolm X, and the Black Muslim World**. New York, NY: Signet Books, 1964.
   This is a biography of Malcolm X, along with a chronicle of his rise to power in the Nation of Islam. Included are reports on Elijah Muhammad and the birth and growth of the Black Muslim Movement. The last chapter is an interview with Malcolm X by the author.
   > BP222 L6 1997
   > LC6321624

6. Muhammad, Elijah. **Message to the Black Man in America**. Chicago, IL: The Final Call, Inc., 1997.
   Originally published in 1965, Elijah Muhammad offers black Americans a new way of life along with "*identification, definition, and belonging*" to all who seek it. Muhammad promotes the transformation of black people in America and offers new ways of eating, thinking, praying, and living in America. This work continues to be popular and widely read among African-Americans within and outside of the Nation of Islam.
   > BP222 .E4
   > 1884855148

BLACK PANTHER PARTY

1. Brown, Elaine. **A Taste of Power: A Black Woman's Story**. New York, NY: Anchor Books, 1994.
   The autobiography of Elaine Brown tells the story of "*the only woman to lead a revolutionary party in the United States.*" Brown tells of her life as a child in Philadelphia and as a young adult flirting with the high and fast life of Hollywood. She chronicles her awakening to Black Power politics and her rise and fall in leadership in the Black Panther Party (BPP). Brown gives insight on the BPP methods of community outreach, recruitment, and struggles for survival. Moreover, Brown confronts the issues of female and male roles and relationships within the BPP movement throughout its various branches in California and elsewhere. The book examines "*one woman's struggle to survive and transform structures despite contending forces.*"
   > E185.97 .B866 A3 1994
   > 0385471076

2. Cleaver, Eldridge. **Soul on Ice**. New York, NY: McGraw-Hill, 1968.

> This collection of letters and autobiographical essays about the life of Eldridge Cleaver, an influential member of Oakland, California's Black Panther Party written by him while imprisoned. This work provides insight into Cleaver's political ideology, personality and character.
>
> E185.97 .C6 A6
> LC67-27277

3. Foner, Philip. **The Black Panthers Speak**. New York, NY: Da Capo Press, 1995.

> Originally published in 1970, this study of Black Panther philosophy includes a chronology of community activities and excerpts from *The Black Panther* newspaper and court proceedings involving Bobby Seale and Huey P. Newton. Speeches and writings from Fred Hampton, David Hilliard, Huey P. Newton, Bobby Seale and Black Panther women such as Joan Bird, Kathleen Cleaver, Connie Matthews and Afeni Shakur are included. Classic illustrations by Emory Douglas, a poem by Erica Huggins, interviews with various journalists, *The Black Panther Party Platform and Program*, *Rules of the Black Panther Party*, and the *Black Panther National Anthem* composed by Elaine Brown, appendix and notes are also included. Also included is a new foreword by Claybourne Carson.
>
> E185 .615 F58 1995
> 0306806274

4. Hilliard, David and Cole, Lewis. **This Side of Glory: The Autobiography of David Hilliard and the Story of the Black Panther Party**. Boston, MA: Little Brown and Company, 1993.

> This work is an autobiographical firsthand account of the Black Panther Party by David Hilliard, Chief of Staff for the Black Panther Party, Oakland, California chapter. Hilliard provides information on the administrative and fundraising techniques used by the Black Panthers. Included in this book are firsthand accounts of Huey Newton's shootout with Oakland police and the murder of Chicago Panther Leader Fred Hampton. Many eyewitness accounts are included in this autobiography. Photos are included.
>
> E185.97 .H55 A3 1993
> 155652384X

5. Seale, Bobby. **Seize the Time: The Story of the Black Panther Party and Huey P. Newton**. New York, NY: Random House, 1970.

> This book is written from tape recordings made by Black Panther Party co-founder Bobby Seale between the fall of 1968 and winter of 1969-1970 to provide a look at the internal structure of the Black Panther Party. This work was originally a series of articles in *Ramparts* magazine.
>
> E185.615 .S37
> LC74-155816

BLACK STUDIES, AFRICANA STUDIES

1. Anderson, Talmadge. **Black Studies: Theory, Method and Cultural Perspectives**. Pullman, WA: Washington University Press, 1990.

> This is a collection of "*essays designed to help make both teaching and learning about the African-American and African experiences resourceful and relevant to the unresolved issues and problems of race that still exist in American society.*" The major topics covered are: "Research Methodology and Approaches in Black Studies," "Topics and Issues in African and African-American History," "Sociological Perspectives and Essays," "Psychology and the Afrocentric Ethos," "Blacks and the Politics of Race in America," "Black Economic Perspectives," and "Music and Dance of African-Americans."
>
> E185 .B583 1990
> 0874220742

2. Asante, Molefi Kete. **The Afrocentric Idea**. Philadelphia, PA: Temple University Press, 1987.
Afrocentricity is described as a concept of being "*African-centered*" in one's personal psychological orientation, i.e., to be African in all one does, thinks, and creates. The author compares European ideologies with African ideologies and reports that the communal nature of African ideologies is more beneficial to society than European "*exclusiveness*." The author calls for a critical evaluation of all social phenomena from an Afrocentric perspective. The author introduces new terminology to best describe Afrocentricity and the study of African concepts and African themes found in the Americas and the West Indies.
DT14 .A78 1987
0877224838

3. Asante, Molefi Kete. **Afrocentricity**. Trenton, NJ: Africa World Press, Inc., 1988.
This third edition is an enlarged and revised book on the philosophy of Afrocentricity. Defined generally as Pro-African thought and action, the concept of Afrocentricity is "*African genius and African values created, reconstructed, and derived from our history and experience in our best interests*." The Afrocentric personality is described as bold and intelligent with an acute awareness of self, perception of others, and the universe from an Afrocentric perspective. The concept of Afrocentricity is linked to African scholars such as Cheikh Anta Diop, Maulana Karenga and Jacob Carruthers. The book is organized into four chapters and has a glossary and references, but no index.
DT15 .A79 1988
0865430675

4. Azevedo, Mario. **Africana Studies: A Survey of Africa and the African Diaspora**. Durham, NC: Carolina Academic Press, 1993.
This textbook provides an overview of Africa and the diaspora examining the link between African and African-American and Afro-Caribbean studies. Designed for college freshmen and sophomores, this work presents the "*experiences and contributions of Blacks in Africa, the Americas, and other parts of the world, from the earliest times to the present*."
DT16.5 .A35 1998
0890896550

5. Harris, Joseph E. and Hansberry, William Leo. **Africa and Africans as Seen by Classical Writers**. Washington, DC: Howard University Press, 1981.
This work is a two-volume collection of essays created from the private papers of Howard University professor William Leo Hansberry, a pioneer in the area of African studies. Hansberry is considered the "*Father of African studies*" and he is accredited with building the foundation for the systematic study of African history, politics, and culture.
DT21 .H28
0882580892

6. Holloway, Joseph E. **Africanisms in American Culture**. Bloomington, IN: Indiana University Press, 1991.
This collection of ten essays provides a comprehensive examination of Africanisms in America, particularly the United States, from historical, linguistic, religious and artistic perspectives. The contributors are Molefi Kete Asante, George Brandon, Margaret Washington Creel, Robert L. Hall, Joseph E. Holloway, Portia K. Maultsby, Jessie Gaston Mulira, John Edward Phillips, Beverly L. Robinson, and Robert Farris Thompson.
E185.A26 1990
025332839X

7. Karenga, Maulana. **Introduction to Black Studies**. Los Angeles, CA: University of Sankore Press, 1993.

> Published since 1982, this text has emerged as one of the standards used in introductory courses of African-American studies. In nine chapters, the author outlines the origins and relevance of the discipline as well as provides a survey of the development of black studies in the seven basic subject areas: history, religion, social organization, politics, economics, black creative production and black psychology.
>
> E185 K27 1993
> 0943412005

CIVIL RIGHTS MOVEMENT-UNITED STATES

1. Berman, William C. **Politics of Civil Rights in the Truman Administration**. Columbus, OH: Ohio State University, 1970.

> The purpose of this study is to *"reconstruct and analyze the origins and development of the Truman Administration's Civil Rights program"* to examine the *"impact of the Truman Civil Rights initiatives on the internal politics of the Democratic party, and to assess and evaluate the contributions"* made by the Truman administration on behalf of black efforts to achieve freedom and justice in American society. A conclusion, bibliography and an index are included.
>
> JC599.U5
> 0814201423

2. Carson, Clayborne. **In Struggle: SNCC and the Black Awakening in the 1960's**. Cambridge, MA: Harvard University Press, 1981.

> This work presents a history of the most influential student organization to emerge from the civil rights movement. Organized in three chapters, the author presents the birth, development and eventual demise of SNCC and the decline of black radicalism in the 1970s. The author states, *"By observing the SNCC's tentative responses to complex dilemmas, we can perhaps gain a new sense of responsibility for our personal and collective fates."* Illustrations, an epilogue, notes, and an index are included.
>
> E185.92 .C37 1981
> 0674447255

3. Carson, Clayborne. **The Eyes on the Prize Civil Rights Reader: Documents, Speeches, and Firsthand Accounts from the Black Freedom Struggle, 1954-1990**. New York, NY: Viking Press, 1991.

> This work is a thorough examination of the civil rights movement in the United States from its beginning in Alabama. This book serves as a companion to the television documentary series by the same name. It includes illustrations and an index.
>
> E185.61 .E95 1991
> 0670842176

4. Harding, Vincent. **There is a River: The Black Struggle for Freedom in America**. New York, NY: Vintage Books, 1983.

> This exhaustive history is told in sixteen chapters beginning with the arrival of Africans on the shores through the end of Reconstruction. The author makes extensive use of period illustrations presenting rare images, such as slave ship rebellions, the Christiana rebellion, masthead of *The Liberator* featuring the story of Nat Turner, and individuals such as Henry Bibb, the leader of the free African community in Canada, and Martin Delany, a physician and black nationalist. Notes, a bibliography and an index are included.
>
> E185.615 .H28 1983
> 0394711483

5. King, Martin Luther, Jr. **<u>Stride Toward Freedom: The Montgomery Story</u>**. San Francisco, CA: Harper & Row, 1958.

   The acknowledged leader of the civil rights movement presents an analysis of the protest movement in Montgomery, Alabama and its meaning for the entire country. A chronology, appendix of formal lists of committee members associated with protest activities in Montgomery, and an index are included.

   E185.89 T8K5
   0062504908

6. Raines, Howell. **<u>My Soul Is Rested: Movement Days in the Deep South Remembered</u>**. New York, NY: Penguin Books, 1983.

   This chronology of the civil rights movement begins with Mrs. Rosa Parks' arrest in Montgomery in 1955 and ends with the death of Dr. Martin Luther King in 1968. This work includes firsthand narratives from participants during the civil rights movement; individuals such as Ruby Hurley who speaks of the last time she saw Medgar Evers alive and Julian Bond who writes of his experience with police during a demonstration in Atlanta. Other contributors include Willie Bolden, an organizer with Southern Christian Leadership Conference (SCLC) organizer; Hartman Turnbow, a black Delta farmer who assisted with voter registration; Mary Curry, Joseph Lowery and many other known and unknown participants.

   E185.R235
   0140067531

7. Young, Andrew. **<u>An Easy Burden: The Civil Rights Movement and the Transformation of America</u>**. New York, NY: Harper Collins, 1996.

   Young traces the evolution from the philosophy of accommodation of the previous generation to the non-violent, direct-action approach of Martin Luther King, Jr. This book also includes a plan for America in its role as a world standard-bearer for freedom, peace and prosperity. This book is a first-person account of the *"brave and the foolhardy, the weak and the strong, the blind and the visionary,"* who fought on both sides of the civil rights movement.

   E840.8.Y64
   0060928905

8. Zinn, Howard. **<u>SNCC: The New Abolitionists</u>**. Boston, MA: Beacon Press, 1964.

   This book is a collection of first hand accounts and essays on the activities of college students participating in SNCC (Student Non-Violent Coordinating Committee) voter registration and education programs in Mississippi, Alabama and Georgia during 1963 and 1964. It contains eleven chapters filled with details of "white backlash," police harassment, and assault. Most significant are three chapters chronicling activity in Mississippi, which is labeled to have been the most dangerous region for SNCC. This work is dedicated to Ella Baker, SNCC adviser, who is described by the author as the *"most tireless, most modest, the wisest activist I know."*

   E185.61Z49 1965
   LC64-20493

ECONOMICS-AFRICA

1. Ake, Claude. **Revolutionary Pressures in Africa**. London, UK: Zed Press, 1978.

This book is an examination of the social forces in Africa to assess whether these forces are moving toward socialist revolution or "*aiding the consolidation of the status quo.*" Initially, the author examines the global production system, the class struggle and the mutual alienation of each class caused by the global production system. He also addresses Africa's continuing dependence upon former colonial rulers and Africa's interaction with domestic and international forces. A critique of the contemporary class structure in Africa is provided to illustrate that the dynamics of class relations do not foster increased development.

      HX439.A37
      0905762142

2. Diop, Cheikh Anta. **Black Africa: The Economic and Cultural Basis for a Federated State**. Trenton, NJ: African World Press, 1987.

This visionary document calls for a unified African state and the promotion of an industrialization program to harness the "*immense sources of energy*" of Africa to fuel the process of development for the entire continent. Arranged into three substantial parts, the author "*explains why attempts at economic development and cooperation can not succeed apart from political unification of black Africa.*" Part one calls for the restoration of African historical consciousness, which proposes linguistic and political unity among the countries. Part two is a compendium of energy sources that provides analyses of energy resources and their production potential for Africa. For instance, the author writes, "*harnessing the hydroelectric power of the Zaire Basin alone could supply all of the black continent with electricity.*" Part three concentrates on the industrialization of black Africa according to where raw materials are present in the eight natural zones that overlap existing politically drawn borders. This is a new expanded edition translated by Harold Salemson, which includes a rare interview with Diop conducted by Cuban political analyst Carols Moore.

      HC800.D5413 1987
      0865430586

3. Rodney, Walter. **How Europe Underdeveloped Africa**. Washington, DC: Howard University Press, 1974.

This book is an examination of geographical, social, political and economic conditions and activities that has resulted in Africa's status as "underdeveloped." This work begins with a definition of "development" followed by five chapters focusing on Africa's underdeveloped economy and technical stagnation and what lead to it. There is a postscript by Professor A.M. Babu, which surmises, "*Foreign investment is the cause, and not the solution, to [Africa's] economic backwardness.*" No index or bibliography is included.

      HC502.R633 1974
      0882580132

ECONOMICS-UNITED STATES

1. Allen, Robert. **Black Awakening in Capitalist America: An Analytic History**. Garden City, NY: Anchor Books, 1990.

Originally published in 1969, this study maintains that black America is essentially an oppressed "*semi-colony of the United States*" and the status of black people in America will not change until this issue is addressed. "Black people cannot afford a system which creates privileged classes within an already super-exploited and underprivileged community." The author provides sound analyses based on historical facts to uncover what he calls a "*masquerade of American democracy.*"

      E185.615.A66 1990
      0385077181

2. Cross, Theodore. **The Black Power Imperative: Racial Inequality and the Politics of Non-Violence**. New York, NY: Faulkner, 1984.

>Twelve years in the making, this study contends that black people in the United States have been systematically blocked from participating in all aspects of society. Of permanent "*outcast*" or "*minority*" status, the study illustrates how racial discrimination (private and public) has "*arrested the economic development*" of black people and "*suppressed their capacity to attain those powers and liberties necessary for success in a competitive economy.*"
>
>>E185.8 C93 1984
>>0916631001

3. Hutchinson, Earl Ofari. **The Myth of Black Capitalism**. London, UK: Monthly Review Press, 1970.

>The author describes black business development in capitalist systems as "*mass self-delusion.*" He writes that black people have the weakest commercial tradition of any group in the U.S. The author contributes this weakness to the African ethnic principle of communalism and its direct conflict with capitalism. The author discusses this contradiction and offers solutions to place black capitalism in "*the proper perspective and reject them once again.*"
>
>>E185.8 O35
>>LC70-105313

4. Marable, Manning. **How Capitalism Underdeveloped Black America: Problems in Race, Political Economy, and Society**. Boston, MA: South End Press, 1983.

>This thesis explains, in ten chapters and three parts, how capitalism has developed mainly because of the brutal exploitation of blacks initially as slaves, then workers and consumers. The author points out that the only time "*black employment approached 100% was during slavery and since WWII the number of black unemployment has soared.*" The author asserts that the "*underdevelopment of black America will end only when black men begin to seriously challenge and uproot the patriarchal assumptions and institutions which still dominate black civil and political society.*" Footnotes, tables, an index and a biographical note about the author are included.
>
>>E185.8.M2 1983
>>0896081656

5. Wolters, Raymond. **Negroes and the Great Depression: The Problem of Economic Recovery**. Westport, CT: Greenwood Publishing Co., 1970.

>This book is an analysis of the impact of New Deal programs—the Agricultural Adjustment Act and the National Industrial Recovery Act of 1933—on black farm and industrial workers. The author concludes that, although black leaders and organizations occasionally were successful in securing relief from flagrant discrimination, they were not able to compel the Roosevelt administration to structure its Economic Recovery Program so that a fair portion of the government benefits would seep down to the masses of black farmers and workers. Notes and an index are included.
>
>>E185.6
>>0837123410

EDUCATION-UNITED STATES

1. Anderson, James D. **The Education of Blacks in the South, 1860-1935**. Chapel Hill, NC: University of North Carolina Press, 1988.

> The introduction states the author's intent as the story of "*the unique system of public and private education that was developed by and for black southerners between 1860 and 1935.*" This book examines both the "*ideological and institutional nature of schooling*" in the black South and "*the interplay of both into education of an oppressed class of America citizens.*" Notes, illustrations and an index are included.
>
> LC2802 .S9 A53 1988
> 0807807937

2. Bullock, Henry Allen. **A History of Negro Education in the South: From 1619 to the Present**. Cambridge, MA: Harvard University Press, 1967.

> This work is a study of the historical development of educational opportunities for blacks in the South and how these opportunities facilitated school desegregation of the 1960s.
>
> LC2801.B9
> LC67-20873

3. Butchart, Ronald E. **Northern Schools, Southern Blacks, and Reconstruction: Freedmen's Education, 1862-1875**. Westport, CT: Greenwood Press, 1980.

> This study examines the early conflicts regarding the form and content of education for blacks. It includes tables denoting secular and ecclesiastical Freedmen's Aid societies from 1862 through 1875. Extensive notes, a bibliography and an index are included.
>
> LC2802 .S9 B87
> 0313220735

4. Du Bois, W. E. B. **Education of Black People: Ten Critiques, 1906-1960**. New York, NY: Monthly Review Press, 1973.

> This collection of seven essays addresses the educational needs and challenges of black people in the United States. Most of these were written during the 1940s and were unpublished until 1973. Included are inspirational essays related to personal hardship and the pursuit of excellence in education. Du Bois also speaks on the "Function of the Negro State University" (1933) and the "Failure of the Negro State University" (1946).
>
> LC2781.D82
> 1583670424

5. Edwards, Harry. **Black Students**. New York, NY: Free Press, 1976.

> This work is dedicated to the spirit of black students who fought for the institutionalization of black studies programs and departments on white college campuses in the United States. It includes comments from students regarding racism on white campuses and the need for black studies to make education relevant to their world experience. Photographs of student activists at Nashville sit-ins and demonstrations at Cornell, Northwestern, Southern, Howard and Columbia Universities are also included. An appendix, black studies curricula, outlines and an index are included.
>
> LC2801.E3
> LC79-116809

6. Harlan, Louis R. **Booker T. Washington: The Making of a Black Leader, 1856-1901**. New York, NY: Oxford University Press, 1972.

> This is an analytical biography of one of the most controversial leaders of black America. The author notes that it is an attempt to understand Washington by his own experiences and his activities as a leader and educator through 1901. The biography reveals Washington privately financed legal efforts to destroy segregation, peonage and other forms of economic discrimination and racism that prevented black people from improving their status in America just after slavery was abolished.
>
> > E185.97.W4 H37
> > LC72-77499

7. Kunjufu, Jawanza. **Countering the Conspiracy to Destroy Black Boys**. Chicago, IL: African-American Images, 1982.

> The author describes how black boys are systematically programmed for failure so that when they become adults they pose little danger to the status quo. Kunjufu cites the public school system as the "*most flagrant*" culprit. He offers in-class solutions and teaching strategies to counter the process *of "de-humanization of African-American children."* There are two volumes.
>
> > LC2771
> > 0913543004

8. Wilson, Amos N. **The Developmental Psychology of the Black Child**. New York, NY: Afrikan InfoSystems, 1992.

> This book is a careful examination of the development of the black child to reveal and discuss "*critical differences between black and white children.*" The author points out the influences that prenatal care, birth weight and early child nutrition and other factors have on development. Created as a handbook for practitioners, the purpose of this book is to strengthen the professionals and the methods used to "*meet more successfully the challenge of black people.*" It includes bibliographical references and an index.
>
> > E185.86.W755
> > OCLC5291999

9. Woodson, Carter G. **The Mis-Education of the Negro**. Trenton, NJ: African World Press.

> In 1933, a New York Times reviewer commented: "*This is a challenging book. It throws down the gauntlet to those who have had anything to do with Negro education, whether of white or black race, and it bids the Negro to come forward in pride of race and heritage and, standing on the basis of his own racial personality, demand an education that will develop that personality and its gifts rather than seek merely to imitate the white.*" Woodson's frank examination of the lack of quality education afforded black children continues to be a popular text on college campuses and in the black community since it first appeared.
>
> > LC2801.W6 1990
> > 086543171

HARLEM RENAISSANCE

1. Bontemps, Arna. **The Harlem Renaissance Remembered; Essays, Edited, with a Memoir**. New York, NY: Dodd, Mead and Company, 1972.

> This memoir of the Harlem Renaissance period, edited by Bontemps, contains essays on key personalities and their influence on the literary period. Artists featured in the essays are: Jessie Fauset and Nella Larsen, Wallace Thurman, Claude McKay, Jean Toomer, Langston Hughes, Countee Cullen, Frank Horne, Charles S. Johnson, and Zora Neale Hurston. It includes illustrations of Arna Bontemps, Rudolph Fisher and Harold Jackson. Notes, a bibliography and an index are included.
>
> > PS153.N5 B63
> > 0396065171

2. Byrd, Rudolph P. **Generations in Black and White: Photography by Carl Van Vechten from the James Weldon Johnson Memorial Collection**. Athens, GA: University of Georgia, 1993.

> This work features a collection of photographs taken by Van Vechten during the Harlem Renaissance and later. This collection features photographs of many emerging black artists in the 1920s through the 1950s.
>
> E185.96 .V36 1993
> 0820315583

3. Cruse, Harold. **The Crisis of the Negro Intellectual**. New York, NY: William Morrow, 1967.

> This work is a scholarly analysis of social and civic life in Harlem in the 1940s. The author examines the influences of politics and intergroup conflict upon the major intellectual leaders of the day. The rise of economic nationalism and the issue of communism in U.S. society and their effect on the theoretical and political activities of black intellectuals in Harlem are examined in detail. The legacy of Marcus Garvey, intergroup conflict, and the struggle between the integrationists and the nationalists are also candidly discussed.
>
> E185.82 .C74
> OCLC225483

4. Huggins, Nathan Irvin. **Voices from the Harlem Renaissance**. New York, NY: Oxford University Press, 1995.

> This collection of essays and literary excerpts highlights the major artists of the Harlem Renaissance. Arranged in three sections, the text begins with a collection of essays explaining the "New Negro Radicalism" as espoused by W.E.B. Du Bois, Marcus Garvey, Asa P. Randolph and W. A. Domingo. Section two is filled with excerpts from Harlem Renaissance personalities including Arthur A. Schomburg, James Weldon Johnson, Jean Toomer, Alain Locke, Sterling Brown, Helene Johnson, Nancy Cunard, Waring Cuney, George S. Schuyler and others. Section three, *"Reflections on the Renaissance and Art for a New Day,"* includes excerpts from Dorothy West, Richard Wright, Claude McKay, Carl Van Vechten, and Langston Hughes.
>
> PS509.N4 V6 1994
> 0195093607

5. Hurston, Zora Neale. **Their Eyes Were Watching God**. New York, NY: HarperCollins Publishers, Inc. 1998.

> Originally published in 1937, this work is the most praised and recognized work by a talented writer and anthropologist of the Harlem Renaissance period. Hurston's writings capture the folkways of the first generation of blacks to leave southern farm life for life in the growing urban centers of the north. This edition contains a forward by Mary Helen Washington.
>
> PS3515.U789 T4 1937
> 0060931418

6. Lewis, David Levering. **The Portable Harlem Renaissance Reader**. New York, NY: Penguin Books, 1995.

> This edition is a collection of well-known writers from the period including: W. E. B. Du Bois, Carter G. Woodson, W. A. Domingo, Marcus Garvey, Mary White Ovington, James Weldon Johnson, Alain Locke, Joel A. Rogers, Paul Robeson, Arthur A. Schomburg, Elise Johnson McDougald, Langston Hughes, George S. Schuyler, J.W. Johnson, Rudolph Fisher, Aaron Douglas, Albert C. Barnes, Romare Bearden, Zora Neal Hurston, Claude McKay, E. Franklin Frazier, Louise Thompson Patterson, Richard Wright, Charles S. Johnson, Gwendolyn Bennet, Arna Bontemps, Sterling Brown, Mae Cowdery, Joseph S. Cotter, Countee Cullen, Jessie Redmon Fauset and others.
>
> PS153.N5 P67 1995
> 0140170367

7. Locke, Alain L. **The New Negro**. New York, NY: Atheneum, 1968.
An influential book when first published in 1925, this work is credited with defining the new outlook and attitude of black artists and scholars at the start of the literary movement known as the Harlem Renaissance. Characterized by a general rejection of the "minstrel tradition," authors produced works of strong black characters and were somewhat influenced by Marcus Garvey's philosophy of Pan-Africanism and self-determination. *"The New Negro articulates the crucial ideas of a generation in rebellion against accepted beliefs and engaged in racial self-discovery and cultural re-assessment."* It includes an original forward by Locke and a new preface by Robert Hayden, as well as a bibliography.
E185.82.L75 1968
LC68-55749

8. Wall, Cheryl A. **Women of the Harlem Renaissance**. Bloomington, IN: Indiana University Press, 1995.
This collection of critical biographies was produced with input from firsthand accounts from those who knew the writers and from analysis of existing data. It includes excerpts of poetry, prose, and essays. Artists featured are: Gwendolyn Bennett, Maria Bonner, Mary Burrill, Mae Cowdery, Alice Dunbar-Nelson, Jessie Redmon Fauset, Angelina Weld Grimke, Zora Neale Hurston, Georgia Douglas Johnson, Helene Johnson, Nella Larsen, Mary Effie Lee Newsome, and Dorothy West. A bibliography and index are included.
PS153.N53 W33 1995
025332908

HISTORY-AFRICA

1. Ajayi, J.F. Ade and Crowder, Michael. **History of West Africa**. London, UK: Longmans, 1971.
This history of West Africa is written in two volumes. The major focus is state formation in West Africa. Most of the data are the result of "primary research, providing new insights into the interaction between land tenure, agriculture and other economic activities and state formation." Contributors include prominent Africanists, such as E.J. Alagoa, I.A. Akinjogbin, Philip Curtin, Robin Horton, Abdullahi Smith, Ivor Wilks, John Hunwick and John Ralph Willis.
DT475.A76
0582645182

2. Ben-Jochannan, Yosef. **Africa: Mother of Western Civilization**. New York, NY: Black Classic Press, 1988.
This work was produced in 1971 to dispute the *"anti-Africanism"* found in libraries and lecture notes in private and public educational institutions across the United States. It contains an investigative history providing documented evidence that African civilization is the basis of western society, beginning with the training of Greek philosophers in ancient African and Asian traditions. It includes extensive resources to primary resources and classical works of the eighteenth century, rare illustrations, maps, a subject index and annotated chapter notes.
DT20.B4 1988
0933121253

3. Ben-Jochannan, Yosef. **Black Man of the Nile**. New York, NY: Alkebu-lan Books, 1981.
This reprint of the most popular first edition published in 1972, contains much of his research on ancient African civilizations. The author's scholarship does much to discredit "*Europeanized*" African history as distorted and, for the most part, omitted from the study of world history. Ben-Jochanan produces scholarly evidence from an African perspective that provides a balanced presentation of Africa and its influence on the world.
> GN645.B45 1989
> 0933121261

4. Bernal, Martin. **Black Athena: The Afroasiatic Roots of Classical Civilization**. New Brunswick, NJ: Rutgers University, 1987.
Two volumes provide historical evidence that the Greek model of history is based on the ancient model. Volume one discusses what the author calls "*The Fabrication of Ancient Greece 1785-1985*" and the Aryan model of world history. Volume two entitled, "*The Afro-asiatic Roots of Classical Civilization*," advocates a return to the "*revised Ancient model*" of world history where the oldest civilizations of Africa are recognized as the first, most influential, and that the "*native population of Greece had been initially civilized by Egyptian and Phoenician colonists.*" Extensive notes, a bibliography, maps, charts, and an index are included.
> DF78.B398 1987
> 0946960550

5. Boahen, Adu. **Topics in West African History**. London, UK: Longmans, 1966.
This survey of West Africa produced by a Ghanaian professor of history is a result of radio broadcasts of lectures on West African history based on "*unpublished theses, articles and secondary works by other West African scholars.*" It is written for secondary and training schools of Ghana and the general reader. It includes an additional reading list and an index.
> DT471.B53
> 0582645026

6. Bohannan, Paul. **Africa and Africans**. Garden City, NY: Natural History Press, 1964.
This general introduction to African history and culture is fifteen chapters, which are divided into four parts: The New Africa, Ancient Africa, Tribal Africa, and Africa in the Modern World. The author exposes the myths that surround Africa and offers facts about the geography and the people. Slavery among Africans and the European-inspired Trans-Atlantic slave trade is examined. Traditional religions, farming methods, markets and economics are also explained for the general reader.
> DT20.B6
> LC64-10025

7. Browder, Anthony T. **Nile Valley Contributions to Civilization**. Washington, DC: Institute of Karmic Guidance, 1992.
The author is concerned with returning ancient Africa to its premiere place in world history in educational institutions of the western world. "*Egypt, a Nile Valley civilization was already old before Europe was born.*" The author writes that the Nile civilization was a strip of geography that extended over 4,000 miles into Africa and influenced many other civilizations.
> CB245.B76 1992
> 092494403X

8. Coquery-Vidrovitch, Catherine. **African Women: A Modern History**. Boulder, CO: Westview Press, 1997.

   This work presents an overview of the life and culture of African women from early to modern times. The author examines the "*lack of leisure*" and the scant observation given African women in anthropological and medical studies during the colonial period and culminates with a look at the continued invisibility of African women due to their role as nurturers.

   > HQ1787.C6613 1997
   > 0813323606

9. Davidson, Basil. **West Africa Before the Colonial Era: A History to 1850**. New York, NY: Longmans, 1998.

   This book is a survey of West African varied environmental and human geography before the arrival of European colonization. This work was written for the general reader outside of West Africa with the assistance of West African scholars, F.K. Buah of Ghana and J.F.A. Ajayi of Nigeria. Sixteen detailed chapters deal with such subjects as early trading states and empires, ancient Ghana, Mali, Songhai, the Hausa States, Senegambia and the forest kingdoms of the Niger Delta, to name a few. This book is rich with illustrations, photos, maps, a table of comparative dates, and an index.

   > DT476.D35 1998
   > 0582318521

10. DeGraft-Johnson, J.C. **African Glory: The Story of Vanished Negro Civilizations**. Baltimore, MD: Black Classic Press, 1986.

    This story of African history is written by an indigenous West African scholar. The author emphasizes and illustrates the relationship between the northern and southern regions of the continent, providing a perspective unlike that of histories of Africa told from an outsider's viewpoint. The book was originally published in 1954 and challenges, with facts and an extensive bibliography, the idea that Africa was "*primitive*" and "*barbaric.*" It provides an extensive treatment of Moorish civilization in Europe. This study was a very important and influential work, appearing before the rise of the African independence and civil rights movement in the United States.

    > DT20.D44 1986
    > 0933121032

11. Diop, Cheikh Anta. **The African Origin of Civilizations: Myth or Reality**. Chicago, IL: Africa World Press, 1974.

    This is one of three documents researched and submitted by Diop for his Doctorate of Letters from the University of Paris. This work presents "*historical, archeological and anthropological evidence*" to support the theory that ancient Egyptian civilization "*was actually Negroid in origin.*" Originally published by *Presence Africaine* in Paris in 1955, this book was translated by Mercer Cook with the assistance of the author. Extensive illustrations, chapter and biographical notes, a conclusion and an index are included in this edition.

    > DT61.D5613 1974b
    > OCLC31056006

12. Jackson, John G. **Introduction to African Civilizations**. New York, NY: University Books, 1970.

    A scholarly examination of African civilizations and the African origins of civilization itself are presented in this book. In ten chapters, the author chronicles the evolution of African civilizations from ancient Egypt to Zimbabwe, Monomotapa and other kingdoms, the empire of the Moors, Africa and the civilizing of Europe, The Golden Age of West Africa, to the destruction of African Culture. Illustrations, an introduction and bibliographic note by John Henrik Clarke are included.

    > DT21.J26
    > LC75-92360

13. James, George G.M. **Stolen Legacy**. San Francisco, CA: United Brother Communications Systems, 1989.
>Originally published in 1954, the author writes, *"Greek philosophy is stolen Egyptian philosophy."* James maintains that the false worship of Greek intellect must be replaced with knowledge and respect of ancient Africa as the true source of Greek ideals and philosophies. The study includes annotated chapter notes with bibliographic references and an index.
>B171.J35 1989
>0865433615

14. Mazrui, Ali A. and Tidy, Michael. **Nationalism and New States in Africa: From About 1935 to the Present**. Portsmouth, NH: Heinemann, 1984.
>This work presents an analysis of African states following independence from respective colonial powers. A joint effort by the author and co-author, Michael Tidy, examines the effects of colonialism, the role of Pan-Africanism, and western influences on their development. There are twenty chapters beginning with the Ethiopian War, 1936-41, chronicling through WWII and its aftermath. The revolutions of Egypt and Ghana, the growth of political parties after independence, the armed struggle, 1950s-1970s, Afrikaners and African Nationalism in South Africa, nations and leadership in independent Africa, problems of disunity, military rule and military coupes, national unity, reviving African culture, the economy, problems of control and development, African diplomacy, international relations, African states and statehood are all covered. Extensive notes, a bibliography, a list of abbreviations, and an index are included.
>DT30.M339 1984
>0435941453

15. Osae, T.A. **A Short History of West Africa, A.D. 1000-1800**. London, UK: Longmans, 1968.
>Edited by Osae and co-author S.N. Nwabara this text was produced for use in instruction in West African universities. Arranged in two parts, part one "The Western Sudan" deals with the influences on development in the area, an examination and description of the peoples of the western Sudan, the medieval empires, the Songhai empire, the Moroccan invasion of the western Sudan, Bornu and the Hausa States. Part two "The Southern Forest Region" is concerned with the states of the forest belt. The states of the forest belt are Oyo Benin, Dahomey, Bono, Akwamu, Asante, the Ibos, and the Niger Delta states. Part two also covers the West African and European's experience. A bibliography, recommended readings and an index are included.
>DT475.O8
>340077719

16. Van Sertima, Ivan. **Golden Age of the Moor**. New Brunswick, NJ: Transaction Publishers, 1993.
>This work, edited by a renowned Guyanan scholar features historical essays by prominent black historians, such as John G. Jackson, Edward Scobie, Beatrice Lumpkin, and others. Moors are defined *"original black Berbers"* of North Africa. The work maintains that the ancestors of the modern day peoples of the Sahara, the Sahel, are the descendants of the Moors, an African people who left their mark on European civilization and culture. It is richly illustrated with an extensive bibliography, an index and short biographies of the contributors included.
>DT14.J68
>1560005815

17. Williams, Chancellor. **Destruction of Black Civilization: Great Issues of a Race from 4500 to 2000 A.D.** Chicago, IL: Third World Press, 1987.
>Originally introduced in 1974, this book chronicles the role of Africa in world history. Included are essays concerning what the author describes as the *"scholars war on blacks"* and the attempt by European scholars to omit Africa from world history.
>DT14.W53 1987
>0883780305

18. July, Robert W. **A History of the African People**. New York, NY: Charles Scribner's Sons, 1970.
> This story of the peoples of Africa gives an account of the social and political aspects of the past and present. Arranged in two parts, "Ancient Africa" and "Modern Africa," there are twenty-two chapters examining thoroughly all aspects of Africa--the continent (the geographical base and the genesis of man in Africa) and the African people (agricultural revolution in Egypt of early times to problems of modernization). This work is richly illustrated with maps, charts and photos. Extensive chapter notes, a bibliography and an index are included.
> DT20.J8
> LC74-93897

19. Rogers, J.A. **World's Great Men of Color**. New York, NY: Macmillan, 1972.
> This work by lay historian is two volumes of biographies with new bibliographical notes by John Henrik Clarke. Volume one includes biographies of ancient African personalities such as Hatshepsut, Thotmes III, Aesop, Piankhy, Nzingha (Ann Zingha), Chaka Zulu, Cetewayo, Tippoo Tibb, Haile Selassie, Samuel Adjai Crowther and others. Volume two includes St. Maurice of Aganaum, St. Benedict the Moor, John IV of Portugal, Chevalier de St. Georges, General Alexandre Dumas, Toussaint L'Ouverture, Marcus Garvey, Arthur Schomburg, Henry O. Tanner, Paul Robeson and others. It contains illustrations and no index.
> DT18.R592
> LC73-186437

HISTORY-CANADA

1. Winks, Robin. **The Blacks in Canada: A History**. New Haven, CT: Yale University Press, 1997.
> This work presents a history of blacks in Canada from 1628 through 1960 with an examination of the racial attitudes of Canadians. The pre-emancipation immigration of mostly black men, some free and others fugitive, from slavery, caused white Canadian indignation and "backlash." The unwelcoming attitudes and treatment did not prevent antebellum blacks from pursuing a new way of life and acquiring economic success in Canada. Many examples of prosperous black colonies and individuals in Canada are provided in this work.
> F1035 .N3 W5 1997
> 077351631X

HISTORY-SOUTH AMERICA

1. Andrews, George Reid. **The Afro-Argentines of Buenos Aires, 1800-1900**. Madison, WI: University of Wisconsin, 1980.
> This work provides a history of the black population of Argentina's capital city and a general chronology of significant events in race relations in Argentina and Latin America in general. It includes a glossary, a bibliography, illustrations and an index.
> F3001.9B55 A52
> 0299082903

2. Ramos, Arthur. **The Negro in Brazil**. Washington, DC: The Associated Publishers, Inc., 1951.
> A general history of black people in Brazil is presented beginning with the Trans-Atlantic slave trade through the 1888 Emancipation of enslaved African descendants. The founding of the Center of Afro-Brazilian Culture (Centro cultural Afro-Brasilera) in 1937 increased interest in black studies in Brazil. The contributions made by Africans to Brazilian culture and economy are also noted. An index, a bibliography and illustrations are included. Richard Pattee translates this work from the original Portuguese.
> F2659.N4 R34
> OCLC1556821

HISTORY-UNITED STATES

1. Aptheker, Herbert. **A Documentary History of the Negro People in the United States**. New York, NY: Citadel Press, 1990.

     This two-volume collection of documents attests to the experience of black people in the United States from Reconstruction to 1910. Examples of documents included are: "The Revolutionary Period: Early Negro Petitions for Freedom 1661-1726"; "Protest Against Taxation with Representation," 1870; "The Early National Period: South Carolina Negroes Denounce Jim Crow Justice," 1791; "Protest Against Poll Tax," 1793-94; "Gabriel's Conspiracy," 1800; "Buying Freedom," 1815; "Vesey Conspiracy," 1822; "The Abolitionist Era: First Negro Newspaper's Opening Editorial," 1827; "Militant Pamphlets by Black," 1929; "A Negro Woman on Women's Rights," 1827; "Negro Youth Leaders," 1834; "Negro Children Speak," 1834; "Garnett's Call to Rebellion," 1843; "Struggle Against Jim Crow Schools," 1844; "Anthony Burns Tells His Story," 1855; "A Pro-slavery Negro and How Negroes Greeted Him," 1857; "California Schools and the Negro," 1859; "The Civil War Period: Seeking the Right to Fight (Private and Public Efforts)," 1861-62; "Men of Color, To Arms!" 1863; "The Ballot, the School, the Land, 1862-1865." Each of the four sections contains many interesting primary sources. An index is included.

     E185.D623 1990
     0806501677

2. Aptheker, Herbert. **The Negro in the Abolitionist Movement**. New York, NY: International Publishers, 1941.

     The author provides historical evidence to show that black people were first to start the crusade against African enslavement in the United States.

     E441.A6
     OCLC743321719

3. Athearn, Robert G. **In Search of Canaan: Black Migration to Kansas, 1879-1880**. Lawrence, KS: Regents Press of Kansas, 1978.

     This work presents a study of black migration to Kansas during the spring of 1879. Black settlers in the West were common but 1879 represented the last hope for black people to move and settle in a place to call their own. In 1879, the movement to Kansas was unplanned, leaderless, and sudden, unlike earlier resettlements led by Benjamin "Pap" Singleton and others. Many blacks were said to have been eager to flee the South and experience a better life and were not interested in wage relationships with their former masters. Illustrations, extensive notes and an index are included.

     E185.93.K16 A8
     0700601716

4. Bennett, Lerone. **Before the Mayflower: A History of Black America**. New York, NY: Penguin Books, 1993.

     This survey of the history of black people in America is written for the general reader. This work was produced from a series of articles originally published in *Ebony* magazine. It includes a timeline of "Landmarks and Milestones" in black history, bibliographical references, illustrations, and an index.

     E185.B4 1993
     0874502909

5. Berry, Mary Frances. **Long Memory: The Black Experience in America**. New York, NY: Oxford University Press, 1982.

> This work presents an analysis of *"lessons learned by succeeding generations of Afro-Americans about the condition of black people and the strategies needed for advancement...."* Chapter themes examine African origins, slavery and the shaping of black culture, the precarious status of free blacks, family and church issues, the battle for education and others. This edition includes an expanded chronology of significant dates in black American history, 1502-1980, an extensive bibliography and an index.
>
> E185.5.B47
> 0195029097

6. Cheek, William. **Black Resistance Before the Civil War**. Beverly Hills, CA: Glencoe Press, 1970.

> From the outset, the author stresses that the central theme in black American history has been one of resistance against white supremacy and inhumane treatment. The author further illustrates that black resistance did not *"spring up, full-grown and unparalleled"* in the civil rights and black power movements of the 1950s and 1960s but has its origins on the African coast, beginning aboard slave ships during the antebellum movement. The author outlines the resistance inherent in the black American experience in five chapters. No bibliography and no index are included.
>
> E447.C47
> LC74-104865

7. Cohen, David W. **Neither Slave Nor Free: The Freedman of African Decent in the Slave Societies of the New World.** Baltimore, MD: John Hopkins Press, 1972.

> This work is a collection of essays resulting from a symposium devoted to the study of the status of free blacks in the slave societies of North and South America and the Caribbean. This compilation of historical essays provides extensive facts regarding the political status of free blacks and the varying degree of freedom experienced by them. It is an examination of the "freedman's" lifestyle and their economic position in early America from the early sixth century through the nineteenth century. The text speaks of a *"desperate group whose place in the larger society was everywhere ambiguous and increasingly under attack from the eighteenth century onward."*
>
> HT1048 .N43
> 081813743

8. Cox, LaWanda. **Lincoln and Black Freedom: A Study in Presidential Leadership**. Columbia, SC: University of South Carolina Press, 1985.

> This is a revised edition of a 1981 study where the author examines the nagging question of whether or not President Abraham Lincoln has a deep-rooted belief in emancipation and civil rights for blacks. This work presents Lincoln as "emancipator" and examines the limits of opportunity for establishing voting and legal rights for blacks in the South in the 1860s. Chapter notes, a bibliography and an index are included.
>
> E457.2.C84 1985
> 0872494004

9. Curry, Leonard P. **The Free Black in Urban America, 1800-1850: The Shadow of The Dream**. Chicago, IL: Chicago University Press, 1986.

> This book provides a critical assessment of the life of free black people during the first half of the nineteenth century. Organized into thirteen chapters, it contains informative tables, figures related to population of free blacks in cities, percentage of property owners including slaveholding, black women slaveholders, mortality, male/female ratio, etc. Also included are appendices, extensive source notes, and an index.
>
> E185.9.C87 1986
> 0226131254

10. Durham, Phillip. **The Negro Cowboys**. New York, NY: Dodd, Mead and Company, 1941.

> A history of black cowboys and their role in the expansion of the settlement in the American western frontier is presented in this work. Black cowboys also drove cattle across the frontier. Many were excellent horsemen winning several Kentucky Derbys. Durham and co-author Everett Jones point out that descendants of these cowboys are among the first families in California and Oregon.
>
> F596.D8
> LC65-10648

11. Franklin, John Hope. **From Slavery to Freedom: A History of African Americans**. New York, NY: McGraw-Hill, Inc., 1994.

> Originally published in 1947, this survey of African-American history has become a standard college text that is updated periodically by Franklin and co-editor Alfred Moss, Jr. The authors trace the history of the African in America from *"his ancient African beginnings down to the present time."* Extensive bibliographical notes, appendices, acknowledgments, and index are included.
>
> E185.F825 1994
> 0070219079

12. Frazier, Thomas R. **Afro-American History: Primary Sources**. Belmont, CA: Wadsworth Publishing Co., 1988.

> This collection of fourteen primary source documents related to the African experience in the United States includes testimony of "Venture Smith" an African taken from Guinea as a child in 1798; several petitions for freedom, and the proceeding against Absalom Jones and Richard Allen, founder of the African Methodist Episcopal (AME) Church. Documents related to the free black community of early America, Civil War, Reconstruction, legal segregation, and the Great Migration through the contemporary Black Power Movement of the 1970s are presented also.
>
> E184.6
> 0534105300

13. Greene, Lorenzo. **The Negro in Colonial New England**. Port Washington, NY: Kennikat Press, 1942.

> This work is a comprehensive history of the origins of the slave trade in early America. The work also examines the status and varied activities blacks from their petitions of freedom to collective efforts to abolish the Atlantic slave trade, which proved to be very lucrative and popular with socially prominent Puritan families. Slavery created much of the wealth and culture of Boston and Newport, and its development gradually diminished the privileges and rights of free blacks to petition in courts and testify against whites. Bibliography and index are included.

14. Katz, William Loren. **Black People Who Made the Old West**. Trenton, NJ: First Africa World Press, 1992.

> This book gives a history of black leaders and everyday people of the American Western region. Originally published in 1997, this work chronicles in six chapters the roles assumed by blacks in the Old West as explorers, fur traders, early settlers, gold rushers, cowpunchers, lawmen, soldiers and architects of the new frontier. It includes photographs, illustrations, reading list and index.
>
> E185.925 .K36 1992
> 0865433631

15. King, Martin Luther Jr. **Conscience for Change**. Canada: Canadian Broadcasting Company, 1968.
This work is a print collection of five radio broadcasts heard in November and December 1967 as the seventh series of the Massey Lectures represented in honor of the late Vincent Massey, former Governor General of Canada. Speeches include: "Impasse in Race Relations," "Conscience and the Vietnam War," "Youth and Social Action," and "A Christmas Sermon on Peace." This broadcast is available on audiocassette (ISBN: 0660183293).
> E185.97 .K5 A53
> OCLC 48643795

16. Lincoln, C. Eric. **The Black Muslims in America**. Boston, MA: Beacon Press, 1961.
This work presents a study of the Black Muslim movement including the Moorish Science Temple and the Nation of Islam under the leadership of Elijah Muhammad and Malcolm X. The influence of Garvey and the UNIA upon the growth of the movement into a powerful reformer of African-American life is also examined in scholarly detail. The author studies the tensions inside and outside of the Black Muslim movement and observes interactions with Jews, Orthodox Muslims and Christians in the black and white communities in nine chapters. Notes and a bibliography are included.
> E185.61
> LC61-5881

17. Quarles, Benjamin. **Black Abolitionists**. New York, NY: Oxford University Press, 1969.
This work presents a study of the black abolitionists and their pioneering and unique roles in the anti-slavery movement and their commitment to blacks that were still enslaved. It gives a history dispelling the myth of "*black passivism*" and revealing the roles played by black individuals and organizations in the crusade against slavery. The author maintains that the anti-slavery movement could not have had any stronger or active supporters than black advocates who were former slaves themselves. This work includes chapter notes and an index.
> E449 Q14
> LC69-1 7766

18. Quarles, Benjamin. **The Negro in the Making of America**. New York, NY: Macmillan Publishers, 1964.
This popular, scholarly and concise account of dynamic black personalities in American history from early times through the rise of black power, Malcolm X and Martin Luther King in the 1960s was originally published in 1964. This work has been reprinted and has been used as college text.
> LC77-87901

19. Savage, W. Sherman. **Blacks in the West**. Westport, CT: Greenwood Publishers, 1976.
A pioneer in the study of blacks in the western region of the United States, the author endured racial prejudice and discrimination to earn his degrees and expertise in U.S. history. As a young professor, he produced early research on the role of blacks in the "*political, economic, and social development of the trans-Mississippi West*." He writes that the objective of his work is to explain the struggle in the West for racial equality and to appraise the significant contributions black people had made to the emergence of the western United States. It includes an extensive bibliography and an index.
> E185.925 .S38
> 0837187753

20. Thornborough, Emma Lou. **T. Thomas Fortune: Militant Journalist**. Chicago, IL: University of Chicago, 1972.

> Fortune is described as the "*most influential Negro American from the decline of Frederick Douglass to the rise of Booker T. Washington.*" Fortune was an editor of the *New York Age* and is known as uncompromising and militant as a reporter and editorial writer. Fortune was a loyal supporter and defender of Booker T. Washington and his Tuskegee machine. The author reveals that Fortune suffered the scorn of many due to his support of Washington. Fortune's speeches, writings, and surviving correspondence with Washington and his wife provide the framework of this biography. It includes bibliographical notes, illustrations, and an index.
>
> > PN4874.F574 T5
> > 0226798321

21. Van Sertima, Ivan. **They Came Before Columbus: African Presence in Early America**. New Brunswick, NJ: Transaction Publishers, 1992.

> This classic and controversial study documents the presence of Africans in America long before the arrival of Europeans. Originally published in 1977, this work is still considered controversial in the fields of cultural anthropology, linguistics, and forensic science. It includes extensive photographs and a bibliography.
>
> > E109.A35 A38 1992
> > 0887387152

22. Pierson, William D. **Black Yankees: The Development of an Afro-American Subculture in 18th-century New England**. Amherst, MA: University of Massachusetts, 1988.

> This work gives an examination of the process of cultural change to creation among black people in colonial New England. It is written from the "*black point-of-view*" in five parts: (1) African immigrants and black Yankees; (2) forces of enculturation; (3) blending of traditions; (4) celebration of Afro-American culture; and (5) resistance.
>
> > E185.917.P54 1988
> > 0870235869

23. Wright, Donald R. **African-Americans in the Colonial Era: From African Origins Through the American Revolution**. Arlington Heights, IL: Harlan Davidson, Inc., 1990.

> Within this brief examination of Africans in America during the colonial period, the author provides historical detail regarding the status of Africans as chattel slaves from the mid-seventeenth century through the mid-nineteenth century, when slavery existed mainly on large plantations and small farms in the Chesapeake Bay area of Virginia and Maryland and the coastal lowlands of South Carolina and Georgia. Rice and tobacco were the primary cash crops to use slave labor before the spread of slavery to the Deep South, where cotton became the main crop associated with slave labor. This work consists of four chapters: Chapter one, "Atlantic Origins," gives an examination of the slave trade; Chapter two, "Development of Slavery in English North America" covers a concentration of slavery in the New England colonies and an examination of racial prejudice and its relationship to the development of African slavery. Chapter three, "African-American Culture" explores the family life of African slaves, resistance and rebellion, etc., and Chapter four, "African-Americans in the Revolutionary Era." A bibliographical essay, an index, maps and illustrations are included.
>
> > E185 .W94 1990
> > 0882958321

24. Painter, Nell Irvin. **Exodusters: Black Migration to Kansas after Reconstruction**. Lawrence, KS: University Press of Kansas, 1986.

> Originally published in 1976, the author chronicles the experience of free blacks following the end of the Reconstruction period. The "Exodusters" were the ordinary poor blacks who left the lower Mississippi Valley seeking new life and homes in Kansas. This research began as a dissertation and is still a valuable resource in the study of the post-reconstruction experience of blacks in the West. A bibliographical essay, a selected bibliography and index are included.
>
> E185.93 K16 P34 1986
> 0700602887

25. Stuckey, Sterling. **Slave Culture: Nationalist Theory and the Foundations of Black America**. New York, NY: Oxford University Press, 1987.

> This work gives an examination of the slave culture for influences on modern-day black American cultural ways in search of self-identity and racial problem-solving. It includes cultural criticism focusing on prominent and influential historical personalities, such as David Walker, Henry Highland Garnet, W.E.B. Du Bois, Paul Robeson and key issues like cultural reality, the meaning of freedom and the names controversy. Extensive notes and an index are included.
>
> E441 .S97 1988
> 0195042654

HISTORY-UNITED STATES, WOMEN

1. Davis, Angela. **Women, Race, & Class**. New York, NY: Random House, 1982.

> The author, an influential social activist, analyzes three historical movements in relation to each other: the movement for black liberation from slavery to the present, the women's movement, and labor activities in the United States. The author uncovers the race and class bias of each movement and its effect upon membership in each movement. Notes are included.
>
> HT1521 .D38
> OCLC Number: 9820104

2. Giddings, Paula. **When and Where I Enter: The Impact of Black Women on Race and Sex in America**. New York, NY: William Morrow, 1984.

> This book presents a history of black women in the United States from the 17th century to the late 1970s. The author chronicles the experience of the black woman from a black woman's perspective and insight. Of special focus is the legacy of black women in their struggle against racism and sexism in a society where they are viewed as second-class citizens. Prominent women such as Ida B. Wells and Mary McLeod Bethune are examined in detail. The work is organized into three parts entitled: "Inventing Themselves," "A World War and After: The New Negro Woman," and "The Unfinished Revolution." This book includes source notes, a selected bibliography and an index.
>
> E185.86.G49 1984
> 0688146503

3. Hull, Gloria T. **All the Women Are White, All the Blacks Are Men, But Some of Us Are Brave: Black Women's Studies**. Old Westbury, NY: The Feminist Press, 1982.

    This is a collection of recent research concerning the experience and status of black women in the United States as related to feminism and politics. This work includes pedagogical tools such as syllabi, reference texts, journal and media lists for the continued development of black women's studies as a field of study. Contributors are: Michele Wallace, Alice Walker, Ellen Pence, Elizabeth Higginbottom, Jacquelyn Grant, Michele Russell, Constance Carroll, Mary Helen Washington, Ramona Matthewson, Joan R. Sherman and others. Patricia Bell Scott and Barbara Smith are co-authors. Also included is information about the contributors, acknowledgments, and an index.

        E185.86.A4 1982
        0912670924

4. Katz, William Loren. **Black Women of the Old West**. New York, NY: Atheneum Books, 1995.

    This collection of short biographies and photographs features the black woman in the west and the many roles played by black women in and among Native American nations, advancing education, and shaping communities. Some of the women featured include Mary Pleasant and Stage Coach Mary.

        E185.925.K375 1995
        0689319444

5. Loewenberg, Bert. **Black Women in Nineteenth-Century American Life: Their Words, Their Thoughts, Their Feelings**. University Park, PA: Pennsylvania State University, 1976.

    This collection of narratives from nineteenth-century black women concerns their life, religion, family, social and economic activities. The book is arranged in four parts and provides excerpts from women such as Silva Du Bois, Louisa Picquet, Jarena Lee, Ann Plato, Sarah Parker Redmond, Frances Ellen Watkins Harper, Ida Wells-Barnett, Lucy Craft Laney, and Anna Julia Cooper. The life experiences of women are viewed as primary sources of black cultural and family history. In their writings, these women present the black woman as a social advocate for black rights and a believer in the solidarity of humankind.

        E185.96 B54
        LC75-27175

6. Sterling, Dorothy. **We Are Your Sisters: Black Women in the Nineteenth Century**. New York, NY: Norton, 1984.

    This work gives a documentary portrayal of the black women who lived between the years 1800-1880. The author uses first-person testimony, interviews of ex-slave women from government documents and private letters from family and friends to reconstruct a view of what life was like during the period for black women. The book is presented in 6 parts: 1. Slavery Time; 2. Free Women, 1800-1861; 3. The War Years; 4. Freedwomen; 5. The Post-War North; and 6. Epilogue: Women as revealed in their dairies and other writings. Some of the women included are Frances Anne Rollin, Mary Virginia and Rebecca Montgomery, Laura Hamilton Murray and Ida Wells-Barnett. Source notes, a selected bibliography, illustrations and an index are included.

        E185.86 W43 1984
        0393017281

7. Yee, Shirley. **Black Women Abolitionists: A Study in Activism, 1828-1860**. Knoxville, TN: University of Tennessee Press, 1992.

    This is the story of how after "two generations of struggle for abolition and women's rights to which black women had constantly committed all the energies and resources at their command" they were excluded from the "victories" of the Fourteenth and Fifteenth amendments to the Constitution. It is also the story of the tension between the ideal of equality and liberty and the reality in the lives of free black women. Notes are included.

        E449 Y44 1992
        0870497359

LITERATURE-AFRICA

1. Achebe, Chinua. **Things Fall Apart**. Portsmouth, NH: Heinemann, 1996.
   This is the first in a series of works chronicling the colonization of Nigeria by Britain. This novel was first published in 1958 and is set in West Africa at the beginning of colonialism. It represents a social document providing an African perspective and literary record of the colonial experience in an Ibo village in an area formerly known as "Biafra." This expanded edition contains notes.
   PR9387.9.A3 T5 1996
   0435905252

2. Armah, Ayi Kwei. **Two Thousand Seasons**. Portsmouth, NH: Heinemann, 1973.
   In this novel, the author presents an artistic analysis of African life under colonialism and provides much motivation for the liberation of African minds and the African continent itself.
   PR9379.9.A7 T963 1973
   0435902180

3. Armah, Ayi Kwei. **The Beautiful Ones Not Yet Born**. Ghana, West Africa: Heinemann, 1969.
   First published in 1969 by a Yale-educated Ghanaian author who wrote about urban life and government corruption, the author writes of an African man who resists the temptations of corruption and easy living only to lose the respect and love of his family and friends.
   PR9379.9.A7 B4 1969
   0435900439

4. Barthold, Bonnie J. **Black Time: Fiction of Africa, the Caribbean, and the United States**. New Haven, CT: Yale University Press, 1981.
   This is a collection of literature by black writers from Africa and the diaspora exhibiting a common thread that is examined as "*separate aspect of modern literature*." Historical foundation is provided in part one, followed by a study of vision in black fiction critiquing theme and form. The final section includes examples of "fragmentation to redemption" as a literary theme in the works of black writers regardless of geography or gender. Works featured are "Arrow of God" by Chinua Achebe, "In the Castle of My Skin" by George Lamming, "Cane" by Jean Toomer, "Son of Solomon" by Toni Morrison and "Season of Anomy" by Wole Soyinka. Index.
   PN841.B3
   0300025734

5. Dathorne, O.R. **The Black Mind: A History of African Literature**. Minneapolis, MN: University of Minnesota Press, 1974.
   This work presents a historical examination of the linkages between the African oral tradition and the written literature of the African diaspora.
   PL8010.D37 1974a
   0816607192

6. Hughes, Langston. **An African Treasury: Articles, Essays, Stories, Poems**. New York, NY: Crown Publishers, 1960.

> This rich anthology of articles, poems, stories and essays in English is by African authors, journalists, poets, educators, statesmen, and politicians including Tom Mboya of Kenya's independence movement, philanthropist Adelaide Casely-Hayford of Sierra Leone, Mabel Dove-Danquah of Ghana, the first woman to be elected to an African assembly, Cyprian Ekwensi, first modern novelist of Nigeria, and Senegalese poet Birago Diop. Works by popular artists such as South Africa's Peter Abrahams and Nigerian playwright, Wole Soyinka are also included.
>
> > PR9799. H8
> > OCLC272735

7. Laye, Camara. **The Dark Child: The Autobiography of an African Boy**. New York, NY: Noonday Press, 1954.

> This autobiography is of an African boy born in Guinea Bissau, an area formerly known as French Guinea, and educated in French as an engineer. While in Europe, Laye is alone and lonely and writes of home. This book provides insight into the ancient ritualistic society of the Malinke people of West Africa. James Kirkup, Ernest Jones and Elaine Gottlieb are the translators.
>
> > DT543.L312 1954
> > LC54-11726

8. Mandela, Nelson. **Long Walk to Freedom**. Boston, MA: Little Brown & Company, 1995.

> This is the story of the legendary South African freedom fighter, Nelson Mandela. He takes us through his country childhood, law practice in Johannesburg to the events that led him to be a freedom fighter. The struggle leads to an inevitable trial for treason and thirty years of prison. His triumphant return to freedom as President of the new South Africa concludes the volume. Illustrations are included.
>
> > DT1949.M35 A28 1994
> > 0316548189

9. Ngugi wa Thiong'o. **Petals of Blood**. New York, NY: E.P. Dutton, 1977.

> This is the first American edition of this controversial Kenyan author who had produced a popular novel portraying the corruption of modern Kenyan politics and government. This work and other offerings by Ngugi are used extensively in African literary courses. Kiswahili editions are also available.
>
> > PR9381.9.N45 P462 1977
> > 0525485201

10. Niane, D.T. **Sundiata: An Epic of Old Mali**. London, UK: Longmans, 1986.

> This is an epic story recorded from a griot (story-teller, historian) from the village of Djeliuba in Guinea, West Africa. This work gives insight into the culture, customs, and legends of pre-colonial traditional Africa.
>
> > DT532.2 1986
> > 0582642590

11. Oyono, Ferdinand. **The Old Man and the Medal**. London, UK: Heinemann, 1989.

> First published as "*Le Vieux Nègre et La Médaille*" in 1956, The Old Man and the Medal is a notable work dealing with the clash of cultures during the era of European colonial rule in Africa. The English translation (translated from the French by John Reed) reads very well, and preserves the elegant vocabulary and sentence structure of the original French. The novel is an indictment of colonialism, but with a subtle and often humorous approach.
>
> > PQ3989.O9
> > 0435900390

LITERATURE-AFRICA, WOMEN

1. Aidoo, Ama Ata. **Our Sister Killjoy: Or, Reflections from a Black-Eyed Squint**. Reading, MA: Addison-Wesley Publishing Company, 1991.
   > The story is told from the perspective of a young female student from Ghana who travels to Germany where she befriends a local woman. While in Germany, the main character "Sissie" is made to grapple with issues regarding colonialism, race, love and nationality.
   >> PR9379.9.A35 O11
   >> 0582308453

2. Brown, Lloyd Wellesley. **Women Writers in Black Africa**. Westport, CT: Greenwood Press, 1981.
   > This broad survey of the achievement of women writers in Africa is an examination of the growth of the African literary market and the share held by African women writers. Some literary criticism regarding the sexual roles of women in Africa as portrayed by female and male writers, such as Soyinka, Achebe, Semebene and Senghor, is included.
   >> PR9340.B47
   >> 0313225400

3. Davies, Carole Boyce. **Ngambika: Studies of Women in African Literature**. Trenton, NJ: Africa World Press, 1986.
   > This anthology of literary criticism is concerned with expanding the body of African literary creativity to include the works of African women. It is a collection of eighteen essays examining the image of women in the works of major African writers such as Ayi Kwei Aramah, Ngugi wa Thiong'o and Chinua Achebe.
   >> PL8010 .N47 1986
   >> 0865430187

4. Emecheta, Buchi. **The Bride Price**. Portsmouth, NH: Heinemann, 1995.
   > The Bride Price is an insightful novel about the life of the Ibo people of Nigeria, West Africa. The author, a well-known African woman writer, deftly captures the girl's adolescent fragility and power as she struggles to carve out her identity among the dictates of patriarchal Ibo culture. Noted for her multi-layered plots, Emecheta writes with great compassion and knowledge.
   >> PR9387.9.E36 B75 1995
   >> 0435900001

5. Head, Bessie. **A Question of Power**. Portsmouth, NH: Heinemann, 1974.
   > This book presents the life of a woman of mixed heritage in South Africa and Botswana who questions her sanity as the result of mistreatment and abusive words from the school headmistress. The headmistress insinuates that Elizabeth is potentially insane like her mother, presumably because she cohabited with an African man. This calls into question the identity and mental health of Elizabeth, the main character.
   >> PR9369.3.H4 Q456
   >> 0435907204

LITERATURE, CARIBBEAN

1. Dathorne, O.R. **Caribbean Narrative: An Anthology of West Indian Writing**. London, UK: Heinemann, 1966.

> This anthology of excerpts from works by Caribbean writers is for the general reader. Caribbean writers featured are George Lamming, Samuel Selvon, V. S. Naipaul, Wilson Harris, Roger Mais, Jan Carew, Edgar Mittelholzer, and other leading writers. Biographical notes are included.
> > PR9326 D3 C19 1966
> > OCLC10112298

2. Dathorne, O.R. **Dark Ancestor: The Literature of the Black Man in the Caribbean**. Baton Rouge, LA: Louisiana State University Press, 1981.

> This is an examination of Caribbean literature in light of its African influences. The author maintains that the so-called "New World" is a black invention and this blackness or, as he puts it, "Afro-New World," is reflected in the literary culture of the Caribbean regardless of their colonial European affiliations. He continues to point to the works of African-American writers to illustrate the similarity and power of the African influences in the "New World." A bibliography and an index are included.
> > PN849.C3 D37
> > 080710759X

3. Hodge, Merle. **Crick Crack, Monkey**. London, UK: Heinemann, 1970.

> This novel examines the theme of West Indian childhood. The story focuses on the central character and her initiation into the black middle class world and what psychological conflicts appear once she accepts an academic scholarship to study aboard. The character deals with dislocation and a sense of alienation during her stay with relatives in London. Her new experiences cause her to re-evaluate her childhood in the West Indies from an adult perspective.
> > PR9272.9 H6 C7 1981
> > 0435984012

4. Lamming, George. **In the Castle of My Skin**. Ann Arbor, MI: University of Michigan Press, 1953.

> This autobiographical novel concerns the coming of age of a Barbadian male child in a dying rural culture that is rapidly transforming into a new "anxiety-ridden world of the twentieth century" with all its pain and alienation.
> > PR6023.A518 I 5 1970
> > LC53-9014

5. Coulthard, G.R. **Race and Colour in Caribbean Literature**. New York, NY: Oxford University Press, 1962.

> This work is a study of race and color in literature as related to Caribbean social, political, cultural and psychological aspects of life in the West Indies. The role of political struggle for independence from colonial powers often found expression in the poetry and novels of Spanish-and French-speaking areas of the Caribbean. Organized into eight chapters, the first two chapters deal with the anti-slavery novel in Cuba and Afro-Cubanism. The rejection of European culture as a theme is treated in Chapter three. Other themes include: the French West Indian background of the Negritude movement; the theme of Africa; Revolt; the colored woman in Caribbean poetry; and the social and psychological problems of the Caribbean are examined in the remaining chapters. Notes, a list of French and Spanish poems quoted, a bibliography and an index of authors are included.
> > PN849.C3 C63 1962
> > LC62-52572

LITERATURE-LATIN AMERICA

1. Jackson, Richard L. **Black Writers in Latin America**. Albuquerque, NM: University of New Mexico, 1979.

   This literary criticism uncovers and examines authentic black literature of Latin America. The book is divided into three historical periods beginning with "The Early Period," featuring the oral traditions of Juan Francisco Manzano (1797?-1854) and Gabriel de la Concepcion Valdez. Manzano, a slave poet, was the first black to publish a book in Cuba. The second period, 1922-1949, focuses on revolutionary themes and black protest in writings throughout the Caribbean and South America. The final period, 1950-onward, examines contemporary works drawn from themes of black consciousness, group solidarity, identity, commonality of experience and identification with Africa.

   PQ7081.J264
   0826305016

2. Lewis, Marvin A. **Afro-Hispanic Poetry, 1940-1980 - Slavery to Negritud in South American Verse**. St. Louis, MO: University of Missouri Press, 1983.

   The author defines Afro-Hispanic poets as those who "*acknowledge their Black African heritage as being important in their artistic and personal lives*" but who do not necessarily write from a racial perspective. Both Spanish and English translations are provided. Extensive notes and a bibliography are included.

   PQ7552 P7L49 1983
   08262040508

LITERATURE-SLAVES' WRITINGS

1. Douglass, Frederick. **Narrative of the Life of Frederick Douglass, An American Slave: Written by Himself**. New York, NY: Harvard University Press, 1960.

   This book is the autobiography of a prominent leader for black freedom during slavery in America. Told in first person, Douglass chronicles his life as a runaway from an oppressive Maryland plantation to his significant contributions as a leader in the Underground Railroad movement, a vocal advocate for race and gender rights, and a journalist/publisher and leading statesman in U.S./Haitian affairs.

   E449.D74905
   LC59-11516

2. Equiano, Olaudah. **The Interesting Narrative of the Life of Olaudah Equiano or Gustavus Vassa, the African, Written by Himself**. Portsmouth, NH: Heinemann, 1996.

   This book is the autobiography of an African captured during the Trans-Atlantic slave trade. Equiano gives firsthand accounts as to the experiences of Africans before and during their voyage to the Americas. Key issues documented in the book are: African ethnic conflicts, housing and captivity, Trans-Atlantic slave trade, British abolition, family separating, chattel slavery, individual freedom, and religion.

   HT869.E6
   0435906003

3. Jacobs, Harriet A. **Incidents in the Life of a Slave Girl, Written by Herself**. New York, NY: Oxford University Press, 1988.

> Harriet A. Jacobs (1813-97) was a slave in North Carolina and suffered at the hands of a ruthless owner. After several failed attempts to escape, Jacobs made her way North to freedom and eventually reunited with her children. This narrative, one of the few written by black women, describes firsthand the sexual indignities to which black women were subjected in slavery. The narrative also provides details related to the selling and wrenching apart of families.
>
> E444 .J17 A3 1988
> 0195052676

4. Keckley, Elizabeth. **Behind the Scenes, or, Thirty Years a Slave and Four Years in the White House**. Chicago, IL: Oxford University Press, 1988.

> Keckley writes that bondage had taught her to be fiercely self-reliant, persevering, and defiant, though more than one slave master tried to beat her into submission. Having worked as a reputable seamstress for three years while also performing her full-time duties as a slave woman, she finally manages to buy freedom for both herself and her son. The author writes of her experience in the White House as the seamstress for Mary Todd Lincoln.
>
> E457.15.K26 1988
> 0195052595

5. Prince, Nancy. **A Black Woman's Odyssey Through Russia and Jamaica: The Narrative of Nancy Prince**. New York, NY: Markus Wiener Publishing, 1989.

> Described as "one of the few surviving autobiographical accounts of a free black woman in the pre-Civil War North," this narrative provides a firsthand account of the St. Petersburg flood in Russia in 1824 and the Decembrist Revolt the following year. This narrative also provides insight into the organized abolitionist movement and the limited role of black and white women. This is a rich collection of adventure and anti-slavery activity by a free black woman in the early 1800s. It includes a poem written by Prince along with illustrations and an index.
>
> E185.97.P94 A3 1989
> 1558760199

6. Washington, Booker T. **Up from Slavery**. New York, NY: Viking Penguin, Inc., 1986.

> Originally published in 1901 when Washington was recognized as a great leader and spokesman of black people, this book is a chronicle of his evolution from slavery to becoming the founder of Tuskegee Institute and the "Tuskegee machine." Washington notes that "*he tried to tell a simple straightforward story with no attempt at embellishment....*"
>
> E185.97 .W4 A37 1986
> 0140390510

7. William, Wells Brown. **Clotel, or, The President's Daughter: A Narrative of Slave Life in the United States**. Boston, MA: St. Martin's, 1996.

> First published in 1853, this is the first work in American literature to concentrate on black slave women. The title character is a mulatto woman, one of the two illegitimate daughters of President Thomas Jefferson. The author escaped slavery to become a fearless advocate for black freedom and a valuable recorder of the black experience in antebellum America.
>
> PS1139.B9 C53
> 1563248034

LITERATURE-SOUTH AMERICA

1. Chiriboga, Luz Argentina. **Drums Under My Skin**. Washington, DC: Afro-Hispanic Institute, 1996.
   This is a novel by one of the most popular feminist writers from Ecuador. The theme of race and gender figure prominently in this story of a woman of color in Latin America.
   PQ8220.13.H57 B3513 1996
   0939423049

2. Olivella, Manuel Zapata. **A Saint Born in Chima**. Austin, TX: University of Texas Press, 1991.
   Published in 1963 as *En Chimá nace un santo,* the author makes important connections between the frustrations of poverty and the excesses of religious fanaticism. The author, a prominent Afro-Columbian writer, indicts the dogmatic attitudes of religious and civil institutions as a major cause of the creation of local cults through a story about a paraplegic who is saved from a burning building untouched. This edition is translated from the Spanish by Thomas E. Kooreman.
   PQ8179.Z38
   0292776330

3. Ortiz, Adalberto. **Juyungo**. Washington, DC: Three Continents Press, 1982.
   This book was winner of the first prize for novels at the Ecuadorian Concurso Nacional in 1942, the year it was written. The black Ecuadorian writer creates a tale of a proud and passionate thrust for justice. This work contains a note for character development that "*elevates the narrative from a social statement to a literary achievement.*"
   PQ8219.07J83 1982
   089410912

LITERATURE-UNITED STATES

1. Brawley, Benjamin. **Early Negro American Writers**. New York, NY: Dover Publications, 1970.
   Brawley, a Howard University Professor of English, originally published this work in 1935. The purpose of the author is to extend accessibility to students and general readers of the black literary tradition. The work includes short biographies and excerpts from the authors featured. Some of the early authors included are Gustavas Vassa, Daniel Payne, Josiah Henson, and others. Literary forms highlighted include sermons, slave narratives and prose.
   PS508.N3 B7 1970
   0486226239

2. Carroll, Rebecca. **Swing Low: Black Men Writing**. New York, NY: Crown Publishers, 1995.
   This collection of interviews reads like an anthology of America's most talented black male writers. Each contributor describes how the American experience has impacted him as an individual, an artist, and a writer. Included in the book, along with excerpts of their work are Caryl Phillips, John Edgar Wideman, Leon Forrest, Henry Louis Gates, Jr., Trey Ellis, and Ishmael Reed, to name only a few.
   PS153.N5 S94 1995b
   0517599813

3. Chapman, Abraham. **Black Voices**. New York, NY: Mentor Book, 1968.
   This anthology of literature reflects the varied artistic vitality of the black American community. It includes literary works of world famous figures and lesser known authors through a sampling of fiction, autobiography, poetry, and literary criticism. Some authors included are Charles W. Chestnutt, Rudolph Fisher, Ann Petry, Frank London Brown, Diane Oliver, James Bladin, Stanley Sanders, Fenton Johnson, Frank Horne, Melvin B. Tolson, Owen Dodson, Lance Jeffers, Naomi Long Madgett, Mari Evans, John Henrik Clarke and others.
   PS508.N3 C55
   0451626605

4. Chapman, Abraham. **New Black Voices**. New York, NY: Mentor Book, 1972.
   This updated anthology of contemporary African-American literary artists and criticism includes new authors such as Jeanne A. Taylor, Ernest Gaines, Nathan Hare, Ishmael Reed, John Oliver Killens, Joe Martinez, Jayne Cortez, Carl Greene, Mari Evans, Michael S. Harper, Stephany, Johnetta B. Cole, Richard Long, and others. Also included are documents such as the statement and purpose of the Institute of the Black World, The Black World Foundation program statement, the purpose of the Black Academy of Arts and Letters and "The Excellence of Soul" by C. Eric Lincoln.
   PS508.N3 N48 1972
   0451626176

5. DeCosta-Willis, Miriam. **The Memphis Diary of Ida B. Wells**. Boston, MA: Beacon Press, 1995.
   This book is a record of the thoughts and activities of one of the most dynamic black women in U.S. history. This edition of her diary provides insight into Wells' early life and work during the late 1880s through the early twentieth century. In addition, Wells writes about her teaching experiences in Visalia, California, Kansas City, Missouri and Memphis during the late 1800s. In addition, she writes of riots, lynching, and attacks against blacks and her journalistic efforts to inspire black leaders to social action to help young black people.
   E185.97.W55 A3 1995
   0807070645

6. Ellison, Ralph. **Invisible Man**. New York, NY: Vintage International, 1972.
   This classic work was widely reviewed and regarded in 1947 when it first appeared, as "*a searing and exalted record of a black man's journey through contemporary America in search of success, companionship and himself.*"
   PS3555.L625 I5
   0394717155

7. Haley, Alex. **Roots**. New York, NY: Gramercy Books, 1976.
   This family history was produced after twelve years of research beginning in Henning, Tennessee, to the Library of Congress, the U.S. National Archives and eventually to the griots of West Africa. Published during the bicentennial year of 1976, this work was serialized for national television and influenced the growth of black genealogical research in the United States. This work is available in videocassette and is commonly used in schools throughout the country. The author is also the editor of "The Autobiography of Malcolm X."
   E185.97H24 A33 1976
   0517208601

8. Hansberry, Lorraine. **A Raisin in the Sun**. Englewood Cliffs, NJ: Prentice-Hall, 1994.
This work is the most celebrated and award-winning play about a first generation urban black family and their attempt to move into a previously all-white neighborhood. Hansberry won the Drama Critic's Circle Award in 1953 for her play, *A Raisin in the Sun*.
PS3515.A515 R3
0679755330

9. Rampersad, Arnold. **The Collected Poems of Langston Hughes.** New York, NY: Knopf, 1994.
This is an extensive collection of poetic works by Langston Hughes, an influential poet from the Harlem Renaissance period. The poems are arranged in chronological ten-year segments beginning with 1921-1930 and ending with the shortest period, 1960-1967 due to Hughes' death that year. Included in this work are a chronology of Hughes' life, an appendix with poems for children, poems circulated by the Associated Negro Press, notes to poems, and indexes to the first line and title.
PS3515.U274 A17 1994
0679426310

10. Long, Richard A. **Afro-American Writing: An Anthology of Prose and Poetry**. New York, NY: New York University Press, 1972.
Co-authored with Eugenia W. Collier, this anthology of prose and poetry is in two volumes. Volume one covers the colonial period through World War I. Volume two includes works from post-World War I period through the Black Arts Movement of the 1960s. Each volume begins with a historical essay of the period highlighted. A biography of the artist is followed by several pieces of their most popular works. Some documents include Jupiter Hammon's "Address to Miss Phillis Wheatley"; Henry Highland Garnet's "Address to the Slaves of the United States." Folklore, tales and sermons, along with Marcus Garvey's "Message from Atlanta Prison"; George S. Schuyler's excerpt from "Black No More"; Gwendolyn Brooks' "Piano After War"; and Ernest Gaines' "The Sky is Gray"; among others. An index of authors is included.
PS508.N3 L6
814749542

11. Major, Clarence. **New Black Poetry**. New York, NY: International Publishers Co., 1969.
This collection of diverse poetry relates the universal concept of liberation and its importance in defining and creating a new black reality. In this collection, poetry is defined as a weapon to fight materialism and capitalism in an imperialist society such as North America. The editor notes, "*Black poets are here to trigger real social change....*" There are 75 poets featured in this work. Contributors include: S.E. Anderson, Ed Bullins, Harry Edwards, Ishmael Reed, John A. Williams, Dudley Randall, John Sinclair, Audre Lorde, Etheridge Knight, Nikki Giovanni, and Quincy Troupe.
PS591.N4 M3
LC69-18879

12. Morrison, Toni. **The Bluest Eye**. New York, NY: Knopf, 1993.
This is the first novel written by Morrison and it is also the most popular and tragic. It is the story of a young black girl in Ohio who longs for blue eyes so she'll be lovable. This work is used extensively in college-level literature courses.
PS3563.O8749 B55 1993
0679433732

13. Porter, Dorothy, ed. **Early Negro Writing, 1760-1837**. Boston, MA: Beacon Press, 1971.

The purpose of this book is to provide access to a selected number of writings by black Americans, which "have appeared in print as books, pamphlets, broadsides, or as parts of books between the years 1760 and 1837." Arranged into seven themed sections, these works represent a historical record of black writings on various subjects affecting the black community. For example, Part IV provides samples of essays and addresses related to emigration. Documents in this section include an 1812 account of the settlement in the colony of Sierra Leone by Paule Cuffe, and "Emigration to Mexico," published in 1832 by a black woman of Philadelphia.

PS508.N3 P6
0807054526

14. Randall, Dudley. **The Black Poets**. New York, NY: Bantam, 1971.

This work is a collection of poetry edited by poet and founder of Broadside Press, Dudley Randall. In this collection, black poets return to their roots and unique life experience to produce poetry that addresses the issues that affect black people in America. Included in this collection are works from forerunners such as black folk tales and spirituals, Phyllis Wheatley, Lucy Terry, Frances E.W. Harper, and Paul Laurence Dunbar. It also includes Harlem Renaissance poets: Arna Bontemps, Langston Hughes, Claude McKay, Countee Cullen, and others. Post-Renaissance poets: Robert Hayden, Sterling Brown, Dudley Randall, Gwendolyn Brooks, Margaret Walker, Margaret Danner; and the 1960s Black Arts Movement poets: Amiri Baraka (Leroi Jones), Nikki Giovanni, Etheridge Knight, Doughtry Long, Don L. Lee (Haki Madhubuti) and others. Recommended readings, list of publishers and periodicals devoted to black poetry are included.

PS591.N4 R32
0553106170

15. Shakur, Assata. **Assata: An Autobiography**. Westport, CT: Lawrence Hill & Co., 1987.

This publication documents the details of the "*carefully orchestrated distortions of fact*" concerning the life and motivation of Shakur that led her to embrace a life of activism. In May 1973, Assata Shakur (Joanne Chesimard), Sundiata Acoli and Zayd Malik Shakur were traveling south on a New Jersey turnpike in a white Pontiac when a New Jersey state trooper stopped them for reasons that have been found to be consistent with FBI COINTELPRO (counter intelligence program) guidelines regarding arresting activists for minor traffic violations. In the scuffle she was shot twice and a police officer was killed. Shakur was charged and spent six and a half years in a maximum-security prison, which she later escaped. She was granted political asylum in Cuba. The introduction is by Lennox S. Hinds, an educator and attorney.

E185.97.S53 A3 1987
0882082213

16. Shange, Ntozake. **For Colored Girls Who Have Considered Suicide When the Rainbow Is Enuf**. New York, NY: Macmillan Publishing Company, 1975.

This work is written as a "chorepoem" depicting the struggles of black American females. Key issues include: life in a male dominant society; the quest for white female acceptance; date rape; loneliness; victim blame; standards of beauty; identity; sexuality; male and female roles; mis-education; survival; and self-definition.

PS3569.H3324 F6 1977
0020248911

17. Walker, Margaret (Margaret Walker Alexander). **Jubilee**. Boston, MA: Houghton Mifflin Company, 1967.

> This civil war novel is told from the perspective of a slave woman. It is a unique novel about slavery and reconstruction in America after the Civil War. The writer reveals that the novel is based upon a story told by her maternal grandmother.
>
> PS3573.A53 1967
> 0553273833

18. Williams, Luis. **Voices from Under: Black Narratives in Latin America and the Caribbean**. Westport, CT: Greenwood Press, 1984.

> This collection of essays from established and aspiring scholars examines the presence of "*Blacks as a unifying force*" in Latin and Caribbean literature. The editor describes the collection as an attempt to "*rescue the black narrative from the fringe of Latin and Caribbean literature and bring it to the forefront of Western literature.*"
>
> PN56.3B55V64
> 031323826X

LITERATURE-UNITED STATES, MEN

1. Abu-Jamal, Mumia. **Live from Death Row**. Reading, MA: Addison-Wesley Publishing Company, 1995.

> The author is a journalist and political activist who writes from a cell on Pennsylvania's death row. This work gives a firsthand account of the author's experience with politics, racism and the death penalty. The introduction is by John Edgar Wideman. Bibliographical notes are included.
>
> HV8699.U5 A65 1995
> 020148319X

2. Belton, Don. **Speak My Name: Black Men on Masculinity and the American Dream**. Boston, MA: Beacon Press, 1995.

> This work is an "*assessment of the intense beauty and dread of physical and spiritual landscapes*" of the black male reality in the United States. A variety of black male writers serve as contributors: August Wilson, Clarence Major, Walter Mosley, John Edgar Wideman, Dany LaFerriere, Essex Hemphill, Quinn Eli, Cecil Brown, Houston A. Baker, Amiri Baraka, Derrick Bell, Dennis Williams and others.
>
> E185.86.S685 1995
> 0807009369

3. Boyd, Herb. **Brotherman: The Odyssey of Black Men in America**. New York, NY: Ballantine Books, 1995.

   This anthology of writings by black men is arranged by theme into six generous sections. Each section has a set of essays reflecting the focus of the theme. The section themes are: 1. Forefathers: "The Griot's Voice"; 2. A Son in the Family with two sub-themes: "Of Fathers and Sons"; 3. Relationships, sub-themes "What's Love Got to Do With It?" and "My Brother's Keeper"; 4. Trouble Man: "The Permanence of Race," "Fighting on Two Fronts," "Locked In and Locked Out," "Color and Class"; 5. Black Magic: "In the Game," "Be Bop, Doo-Wop, Hip Hop"; 6. "Sankofa: 'Past as Prologue.'" Some of the black male writers included are Booker T. Washington, Randall Kenan, Howard Thurman, Quincy Troupe, James Baldwin, Henry Louis Gates, Haki Madhubuti, Michael Dyson, Claude Brown, Henry Dumas, Kevin Powell, Che Tyehimba Taylor, Trey Ellis, Chester Himes, Brent Staples, Essex Hemphill, E. Lyn Harris, Gerald Early, Nathan McCall, Rudolph Fisher, Derrick Bell, Gordon Parks, and many others. This work includes biographies on all contributors. The co-author is Robert L. Allen.

   PS508.N3 B745 1995
   0345376706

LITERATURE-UNITED STATES, WOMEN

1. Bell, Roseann P. **Sturdy Black Bridges: Visions of Black Women in Literature**. Garden City, NY. Anchor Press/Doubleday, 1979.

   This selection of character studies critically examines the images of black women in American literature. The treatment is in three parts: (1) analytical vision; (2) conversational vision; and (3) creative vision. Contributors include Hortense Spillers, Iva Curruthers, Bessie Head, Sonia Sanchez, Margaret Walker, Audre Lorde, Haki Madhabuti, and others.

   PN56.3.B55 S86
   0385133472

2. Cade, Toni. **The Black Woman: An Anthology**. New York, NY: Signet Book, 1970.

   This is an early anthology of works by black female writers and activists in the late 1960s. Contributors include: Frances Beale, Helene Cade, Grace Lee Boggs, Jean Carey Bond, Carole Brown, Toni Cade (later Toni Cade Bambara), Joanna Clark, Ann Cook, Francee Convington, Joanne Grant, Nikki Giovanni, Abbey Lincoln, Audre Lorde, Verta Mae Smart-Grosvenor, Gwen Patton, Pat Robinson, and Alice Walker.

   E185.86 C28
   0451626923

3. Christian, Barbara. **Black Feminist Criticism: Perspectives on Black Women Writers**. New York, NY: Teachers College Press, 1997.

   This collection of analytical essays examines the historical and literary legacies of black women in America. The author explores the images of black women in the literature of Alice Walker, Toni Morrison, Audre Lorde, Gloria Naylor, Paule Marshall and other black women writers. An index and a note about the author are included.

   PS153.N5 C47 1997
   0807762539

4. Cooper, Anna Julia. **A Voice from the South**. New York, NY: Oxford University Press, 1988.
   The prevailing stereotype is that black women were "ignorant and immoral." It is the attitude Cooper attacks soundly in her work of black feminist thought, first published in 1892. The author challenges the prevailing attitudes about black women and takes black men to task for not insisting on the inclusion of black women in gaining higher education and political privilege. The exclusion of Cooper's work from other famous works of this period, dominated by black male intellectuals, is attributed to the fact that Cooper was a black woman writing about black women's issues for reading by other black women.
   > E185.86 C587 1988
   > 0195052463

5. Evans, Mari. **Black Women Writers (1950-1980): A Critical Evaluation**. New York, NY: Anchor, 1984.
   This work presents a critical collection of nationally recognized black women writers. Those included are Maya Angelou, Toni Cade Bambara, Gwendolyn Brooks, Alice Childress, Lucille Clifton, Mari Evans, Nikki Giovanni, Gayle Jones, Audre Lorde, Paule Marshall, Toni Morrison, Carolyn Rodgers, Sonia Sanchez, Alice Walker, and Margaret Walker. An index is included.
   > PS153.N5 B558 1984
   > 0385171250

6. Harley, Sharon. **Afro-American Woman: Struggles and Images**. Port Washington, NY: Kennikat Press, 1978.
   This is a resource in two parts, outlining the historical overview of black women in America. Part one provides a historical overview and part two focuses on three activists: Anna Julia Cooper, Nannie Burroughs and the 1952 Vice Presidential campaign of Charlotta A. Bass. Contributors include: Evelyn Brooks Barnett, Gerald Gill, Sharon Harley, Daphne Duval Harrison, Dorothy Porter, Andrea Benton Rushing and Rosalyn Terborg-Penn. Notes and index are included.
   > E185.86A.34
   > 0804692092

7. Hooks, Bell. **Ain't I a Woman: Black Women and Feminism**. Boston, MA: South End Press, 1984.
   In this landmark book, the author reveals how black women have been victimized by both racism and sexism. This work describes and analyzes their impact on the lives of black women since slavery.
   > E185.86.H73 1984
   > 0896081281

8. Noble, Jeanne. **Beautiful, Also, Are the Souls of My Black Sisters: A History of the Black Woman in America**. Englewood Cliffs, NJ: Prentice-Hall, Inc., 1978.
   This chronology of black women begins with an overview of African origins and the many roles assumed by black women in American society. Composed of ten chapters in three parts, the author examines "the past" status of black women as free Africans, American slaves, "Dishwater Images," the black woman as "servant" and self-sacrificing nurturer. The final section, "Present and Future" examines the black woman as a writer, activist, and as a partner with the black men in nation building. An index is included.
   > E185.86 N6
   > 013066555X

9. Richardson, Marilyn. **Maria W. Stewart: America's First Black Woman Political Writer: Essays and Speeches**. Bloomington, IN: Indiana University Press, 1987.

> A contemporary of black abolitionist David Walker, Stewart was inspired by his courageous writings and embarked on a career of lecture and writings to encourage self-determination and self-help among black Americans. Notes, a bibliography and an index are included.
>
> E185.97.S84 A2 1987
>
> 025336342X

10. Washington, Mary Helen. **Invented Lives: Narratives of Black Women 1869-1960**. New York, NY: Anchor Press, 1987.

> This anthology of selections from eight writers includes Pulitzer Prize winners, Gwendolyn Brooks, Ann Petry, Harriet Jacobs and Zora Neale Hurston. The introduction and first six chapters *"examine with honesty, clarity and insight the critical stages in the struggle to find a narrative structure to accommodate the experiences of black women in this society."*
>
> PS647.A35
>
> 0385183933

11. Wilkerson, Margaret B. **9 Plays by Black Women**. New York, NY: Penguin Books, 1986.

> This work is a combination of the best new plays and their forerunners. The nine plays included are: *A Black Woman Speaks* (1950) by Beah Richards; *Toussaint: Excerpt from Act I of a Work in Progress* (1961) by Lorraine Hansberry; *Wedding Band* (1966) by Alice Childress; *The Tapestry* (1976) by Alexis DeVeaux; *Unfinished Women Cry in No Man's Land While a Bird Dies in a Gilded Cage* (1977) by Aishah Rahman; *"Spell #7: Geechee Jibara Quilk Magic Trance Manual for Technologically Stressed Third World People"* (1979) by Ntozake Shange; *The Brothers* (1982) by Kathleen Collins; *Paper Dolls* (1983) by Elaine Jackson; *Brown Silk and Magenta Sunsets* (1985) by P.J. Gibson. An introduction, acknowledgments and a bibliography are included.
>
> PS628.N4 A13 1986
>
> 0451628209

12. Wilson, Harriet E. **Our Nig: or Sketches from the Life of a Free Black**. New York, NY: Vintage Books, 1859.

> This book is recognized as the first novel published by a black person in the United States. This edition is published with extensive notes concerning verification of the existence of the author to facilitate further research in *"finer detail the curiously compelling story of the life and times of Harriet E. Wilson."*
>
> PS3334.W39O9 1983
>
> 0394715586

MILITARY-UNITED STATES

1. Brewer, James H. **The Confederate Negro: Virginia's Craftsmen and Military Laborers**. Durham, NC: Duke University Press, 1969.

> This work provides a detailed examination of the role of black men in Virginia during the Civil War to assist the Confederacy in war industry and transport. Black labor was used to "close a huge gap in Virginia's technological labor needs." The skill and strength of black laborers were said to be "key elements in the mechanisms of Confederate technology, logistics, transportation, and fortification." Included are notes, bibliography, and index.
>
> E585.N3 B7
>
> 822302047

2. Flipper, Henry O. **The Colored Cadet at West Point: Autobiography of Lt. Henry Ossian Flipper, First Graduate of Color from the Military Academy**. Lincoln, NE: University of Nebraska Press, 1998.

   Henry Ossian Flipper was the first African-American graduate of West Point. His record of accomplishment and personal experience at West Point was first published in 1878. The racism and degradation he suffered is documented in this, his own account of his military career. Flipper was court-martialed and dismissed from the service in 1882 for allegedly mishandling funds. Flipper spent 50 years of his life trying to clear his name. Biographer Charles M. Robinson, III researched military records related to the court martial to recreate events and assess the fairness of the proceedings. His findings indicate that racism and professional jealousy were underlying influences on the decision to court-martial Flipper. A biographical essay is included.

   U410.P1 F6
   0803268904

3. Fowler, Arlen L. **Black Infantry in the West, 1869-1891**. Westport, CT: Greenwood Press, 1971.

   This study was carved from U.S. and state official records documenting the history of black men serving as infantry in the West. Reliance upon official records in most cases was the only remaining evidence of these men, as many were illiterate and did not leave memoirs. In addition to fighting Native Americans, these units installed telegraph lines, built roads, guarded watering holes, and escorted stagecoaches and trains. Ignored by the press and the general public, these men faced prejudice and discrimination both in and out of the army. This work includes rare photographs, illustrations, and index.

   E185.63F66
   837133130

4. Higginson, Thomas Wentworth. **Army Life in a Black Regiment**. Boston, MA: Norton, 1984.

   The narrative of Union colonel Thomas W. Higginson, the commander of the first American regular army of free blacks was originally published in 1870. This work is arranged into twelve chapters and reads much like a diary or journal. Higginson is credited with coining the phrase *"praise the Lord and pass the ammunition."* This edition includes the original preface and a new introduction by Howard N. Meyer, a biographer. An appendix and index are also included.

   E492.941H5 1984x
   0393301575

5. Leckie, William H. **The Buffalo Soldiers: A Narrative of the Negro Cavalry in the West**. Norman, OK: University of Oklahoma Press, 1967.

   This work presents the narrative history of the ninth and tenth Calvary of the United States Army during their years on the Central Plains of the Western United States. Their work was not limited to fighting Native Americans; the labor of these black soldiers was used to lay foundations for future cities. Fort Sill, Oklahoma and Lawton are given as examples. A bibliography, portraits, and maps are included. The portraits are of the white commanders only.

   UA31 10TH .L4
   LC67-15571

6. Scott, Emmett J. **Scott's Official History of the American Negro in the World War**. Westport, CT: Arno Press, 1996.

   Originally published in 1919, this reprint is a complete and authentic narration drawn from official sources concerning the role of the African-American soldier in the first World War. It describes the experiences of black soldiers in Europe and includes many photographs of continental African troops fighting on behalf of European colonial powers.

   E185.63 .S26
   0405018924

7. Wilson, Joseph T. **The Black Phalanx: African-American Soldiers in the War of Independence, The War of 1812 & The Civil War**. New York, NY: Arno Press, 1968.

>This book is a reprint of black men in American wars by Joseph T. Wilson, a Virginia representative during Reconstruction. First published in 1887, this book is recognized as the official history of black soldiers in the American Revolution, the War of 1812, and the Civil War. It is filled with captioned photographs and illustrations of black men and women in the armed forces and the roles they assumed.
>
>E185.63W815 1968
>LC-29023

8. Emilio, Luis F. **A Black Regiment: The History of the 54th Massachusetts, 1863-1865**. New York, NY: De Capo, 1995.

>Used as the basis for the modern film, "Glory," this book was first published in 1894. The 54th Massachusetts was the first black regiment raised in the North. Luis Emilio was the captain in charge of this infantry. It includes maps, illustrations of both black and white officers, and an index.
>
>E513.5 E
>0306806231

MUSIC-AFRICA

1. Bebey, Francis. **African Music: A People's Art**. New York, NY: Lawrence Hill Book Publishers, 1975.

>In the introduction, the author explains the personal and spiritual importance of music in traditional African society. It includes discography and descriptions of instruments from all parts of Africa, illustrations and musical styles related to cultural occasions. Josephine Bennett is the translator of this edition. Index and discography provided.
>
>ML3760.B42 1975
>1556521286

2. Diallo, Yaya. **The Healing Drum: African Wisdom Teachings**. Rochester, VT: Destiny Books, 1989.

>This study of the musical perspectives of the author and the Minianka people of West Africa gives a unique chronology of the author's life and the sacred healing role of music in the Minianka tradition. Music is explained as a "*remedy for both physical and psychological imbalances.*" It includes illustrations and an index.
>
>ML3760.D52 1989
>0892812567

3. Nketia, J.H. **Drumming in Akan Communities of Ghana**. Edinburgh, UK: Thomas Nelson and Sons LTD, 1963.

>This is a study of the social implications of Akan drumming and the role of the drum in Akan society. The author describes the uses of the drum to convey messages as well as provide music for all occasions in musically homogenous groups among the Asante in West Africa. The data was collected from 1952-1956 in Ghana. The appendix includes tables, a glossary, and illustrations.
>
>ML3760.N62
>LC 65-84925

MUSIC-UNITED STATES

1. Abdul, Raoul. **Blacks in Classical Music: A Personal History**. New York, NY: Dodd, Mead, 1977.
   The author, a music critic, describes the contribution of blacks to European classical music in their roles as composers, singers, opera performers, keyboard artists, instrumentalists, conductors and others. The final chapter includes observed attitudes toward black classical performers. Notes and illustrations are included.
   ML385.A27
   0396073948

2. Floyd, Samuel A., Jr. **The Power of Black Music: Interpreting its History from Africa to the United States**. New York, NY: Oxford University Press, 1995.
   This book presents an approach to the study of music based on the fact that "*African musical traits and cultural practices not only survived but played a major role in the development and elaboration of African-American music.*" The author notes that the same motivations influence both African-American and African music. This study is committed to discrediting the concept of "high art" and "low art" as related to black music, such as spirituals and blues.
   ML3556.F65 1995
   0195082354

3. Handy, D. Antoinette. **Black Women in American Bands and Orchestras**. Metuchen, NJ: Scarecrow Press, 1981.
   This study is a history of black women instrumentalists as members of orchestral ensembles rather than soloists or administrators. Data collection methods included personal interviews, surveys of orchestras, secondary sources and compilation of personal data by the author.
   ML82.H36
   0810813467

4. Jones, LeRoi (Amiri Baraka). **Blues People: The Negro Experience in White America and the Music That Developed from It**. New York, NY: William Morrow, 1963.
   This analytical and theoretical examination of black music in America studies how it has evolved and changed as the status, culture and lifestyles of black people continues to change. It is a thoughtful work by literary artist, poet, and social critic Amiri Baraka that is still used in many classrooms in the United States to open discussion on the evolution of black music genres and its influence on American popular music.
   ML3556.J73
   LC63-17688

5. Southern, Eileen. **The Music of Black Americans**. New York, NY: Norton, 1983.
   This historical and cultural examination of the music of black people in America is designed as a college textbook. This work provides an introduction to the cultural art form as expressed by black music makers.
   ML3556 S74 1983
   0393952797

6. Spencer, Jon. **Protest and Praise: Sacred Music of Black Religion**. Minneapolis, MN: Fortress Press, 1990.

> This work presents a study of African-American sacred music and its influence inside and outside of the religious arena. It gives an examination of the holistic nature of black music and the controversial attempt of some scholars to separate the "spiritual" from the "political" experience in African-American music and culture, in general. The author maintains that "*spirituals were unquestionably the archetype*" of all black songs, including the blues, social gospel, and protest songs.
> ML 3556 .S8 1990
> 0800624041

7. Walker, Wyatt Tee. **Somebody's Calling My Name: Black Sacred Music and Social Change**. Valley Forge, PA: Judson Press, 1979.

> This book chronicles a history of black religious music and its role in the black church. The work is divided into eight chapters tracing the development of sacred music in the black church and how this music energized the Civil Rights Movement.
> ML3556 .W23
> 0817009809

8. Work, John W. **Folk Song of the American Negro**. New York, NY: Negro Universities Press, 1969.

> This early ethnography of African-American songs and their meanings written by Fisk University sociologist/anthropologist John Wesley Work was originally printed in 1915. These songs were collected over a ten-year period and represent the earliest forms of black songs in America with roots to various African ethnic groups. The author points out that while tribal life differs in Africa, the focus of their songs is "*wonderfully the same.*" This discovery, he notes, is more important than the differences. The focal of African and early African-American songs recognizes the connectivity of natural forces, God, and man. The author confronts the myths regarding the African-American musical and religious practices and offers readers a scholarly firsthand examination of the diversity and spirituality of the black folk song. This work includes ten chapters, illustrations, music and lyrics of early spirituals.
> ML3556.W78 1969
> 0837127904

PAN-AFRICANISM

1. Cronon, E. David. **Black Moses: The Story of Marcus Garvey and the Universal Negro Improvement Association**. Madison, WI: University of Wisconsin Press, 1962.

> This history of Marcus Garvey was developed from personal interviews with Amy Jacques and Amy Ashwood Garvey, private collections of Universal Negro Improvement Association (UNIA) members and primary source materials housed at the Schomburg and Harvard University libraries. The book is organized into eight chapters and chronicles the rise and fall of Garvey and the mutation of the UNIA. The author offers detailed accounts of Garvey's stormy relationship with prominent African-American leaders such as W.E.B. Du Bois, James Weldon Johnson, and newspaper editors George S. Schuyler and Robert S. Abbott.
> E185.97G3 C7
> 0135560683

2. Garvey, Amy Jacques. **Philosophy and Opinion of Marcus Garvey**. Totowa, NJ: Frank Cass Co. Ltd., 1967.

>This second edition has an introduction by E.U. Essien-Udom, where he provides a historical overview of the Garvey movement and the concept of Black Nationalism. Originally published in 1923, this work was compiled by the second wife of Pan-Africanist Marcus Garvey to keep the "Back to Africa" movement alive while Garvey served five years for mail fraud in the Atlanta Federal Penitentiary. Interestingly, one historical document related to Firestone, Liberia, and the UNIA was confiscated when it was received at the Atlanta prison addressed to Marcus Garvey. This work includes photographs, letters, lists and axioms of Garvey.
>
>E185.97G3 A25 1967
>071462120X

3. Lewis, Rupert. **Marcus Garvey: Anti-Colonial Champion**. Trenton, NJ: Africa World Press, Inc., 1988.

>This is a history of Pan-Africanist Marcus Garvey written by a Jamaican scholar with the assistance of Amy Jacques Garvey. The author makes extensive use of primary materials gained from surviving "Garveyites" from the United States and throughout the Caribbean. Index and bibliography included.
>
>E185.97 G3 L49 1988
>0865430616

4. Martin, Tony. **Race First: The Ideological and Organizational Struggles of Marcus Garvey and the Universal Negro Improvement Association**. Westport, CT: Majority Press, 1976.

>After a brief biographical introduction, the study examines the major features of Garvey's ideological outlook as manifested in theory and practice. The latter portion of the book examines the formidable battles, which the UNIA faced on a variety of fronts: communists, reactionary blacks, powerful governments, and personal animosities within the organization. Extensive notes and an index are included. Also included is an appendix created from UNIA membership cards listing all UNIA chapters and divisions throughout the world.
>
>E185.97G3M37
>0912469236

5. Walters, Ronald W. **Pan Africanism and the African Diaspora: An Analysis of Modern Afrocentric Political Movements**. Detroit, MI: Wayne State University Press, 1993.

>This analysis of modern Pan-Africanism uses many original materials gathered from interviews, travel and solid empirical field research. The author's personal commitment to the subject enables the examination of the *"complexity, richness and significance of the idea of Africa among her peoples throughout the world."*
>
>DT16.5.W35
>0814321852

PERFORMING ARTS

1. Bogle, Donald. **Toms, Coons, Mulattoes, Mammies, and Bucks: An Interpretive History of Blacks in American Film**. New York, NY: Continuum, 1994.

>The third edition of a comprehensive study of the black image in American cinema, originally published in 1989. The history and work of the black actor, actress and filmmaker is chronicled with illustrations from American motion pictures. Some of the themes examined include *Black Beginning: Uncle Tom's Cabin to Birth of a Nation, Jesters and Servants, Entertainers,* and the classic ones: *Mammy, Tom, Coon and the Tragic Mulatto.* Index and illustrations are provided.
>
>PN1995.9.N4 B6 1994
>0826405789

2. Hatch, James Vernon. **Black Theatre USA: Forty-Five Plays by African-Americans from 1847 to Today**. New York, NY: Free Press, 1996.
> This work contains an impressive anthology of black playwrights writing of the black experience. Playwrights represented are Willis Richardson, Randolph Edmonds, H.F.V. Edward, Langston Hughes, Theodore Ward, Owen Dodson, May Miller, Theodore Browne, Richard Wright, Paul Green, Stanley Richards, Abram Hill, James Baldwin, Louis Peterson, William Branch, Loften Mitchell, Charles Sebree, C. Bernard Jackson, James V. Hatch, Douglas Turner Ward, Lorraine Hansberry, Alice Childress, Adrienne Kennedy, Martis Charles, Ted Shine, Imamu Amiri Baraka, Ed Bullins and Val Ferdinand. This text includes a selected bibliography of plays by authors represented and an index.
>> PS628.N4
>> 0684823063

3. Hill, Errol. **The Theatre of Black Americans**. New York, NY: Applause Theatre Book Publishers, 1987.
> This collection of critical essays on African-American theatre is in four parts: Roots and Rituals, the search for identity; The Image Makers, plays and playwrights; The Presenters, companies of players; The Participators, audience and critics. It includes a chronology of important events in African-American theatre, a bibliography and notes on contributors. Contributors include James Hatch, Shelby Steele, Eileen Southern, Larry Neal, Abiodun Jeyifous, and Eleanor Traylor.
>> PN2270.A35 T48 1987
>> 0936839279

4. King, Woodie. **Black Drama Anthology**. New York, NY: Meridian, 1986.
> A collection of twenty-three dramatic works from the late 1960s selected to present a wide perspective of work by black playwrights. The works vary in mood, method, mode of attack, and they range from realism to comedy. Included in the collection is "The Corner" by Ed Bullins, "Brotherhood" by Douglas Turner Ward, "Strictly Matrimony" by Errol Hill, "Mother and Child" by Langston Hughes. Bibliography and index included. Co-author is Milner Ron.
>> PS628 N4 K5
>> 0452009022

5. Patterson, Lindsay W. **Black Theatre: A 20th Century Collection of the Work of its Best Playwrights**. New York, NY: Dodd, Mead, 1971.
> A collection of the "best" examples of varying types of plays written by African Americans since "St. Louis Woman" by Arna Bontemps and Countee Cullen. Some of the twelve plays included are "The Dutchman" by LeRoi Jones (Amiri Bakara),"Trouble in Mind" by Alice Childress, "No Place to be Somebody" by Charles Gordone, "Purlie Victorious" by Ossie Davis, "Ceremonies in Dark Old Men" by Lonnie Elder III to name a few. Index.
>> PS628 N4 P3
>> 0396062547

POLITICAL SCIENCE-AFRICA

1. Boateng, E.A. **A Political Geography of Africa**. New York, NY: Cambridge University Press, 1978.
    This work is an examination of the relationships between the African states and the land they occupy. Presented in two parts and twelve chapters, the author, a Ghanaian geographer, defines and introduces the principles and concepts of "political geography" in chapters one and two. Part two includes the remaining chapters presenting a thorough examination of each African country from the geographical features to their influence on the political, social and economic activities of the population. Chapter twelve provides a history of the Organization of African Unity (OAU) and the evolution of the African independence movement. The appendices contain basic data on African countries (official name, language, designation of citizens, area, population, capital and date of independence). Also included is the OAU charter, a bibliography and an index.
    DT31.B57
    0521217644

2. Clarke, John Henrik. **Africans at the Crossroads: Notes on an African World Revolution**. Trenton, NJ: Africa World Press, 1991.
    These collections of provocative speeches from John Henrik Clarke address Africa's readiness to self-rule. A keen observer of world developments, Clarke analyzes that *"Africans caught in the crossfire of the struggle for world power are learning some painful lessons they should have learned long ago: Mainly, that freedom is not free. Freedom is something you take with your own hands. You maintain it with your own hands. Freedom is not handed down from one generation to another."*
    DT20.C53 1991
    0865432716

3. Davidson, Basil. **Modern Africa: A Social and Political History**. New York, NY: Longmans, 1994.
    This book gives a broad historical treatment with analysis regarding human and economic development and political reconstruction of African states to better manage the continent's many challenges. Part one examines the partitioning of Africa and the changes and developments in Africa during the colonial period, 1914-1930. Part two focuses on the Depression, WWII, and the rise of African Nationalism. Part three deals with the push toward independence and efforts to "de-colonize" African governments. All of the chapters deal with modern questions about development, African unity, and stability. An appendix of key periods and events, 1884-1990, independence dates, recommended reading, and an index are included.
    DT29.D384 1994
    058221288X

4. Du Bois, W.E.B. **The World and Africa: An Inquiry into the Part Which Africa Has Played in World History**. New York, NY: International Publishers, 1965.
    Originally published in 1947 by Viking Press, this study chronicles the role and contributions of Africa to world civilization. Du Bois provides a balance and highly detailed account of Africa and its relationships with Europe in eleven chapters. He draws on the ancient travel records of Ibn Batuta and Duatre Barbosa and early works of modern scholars, such as George Padmore, E.D. Moore, Leo Hansberry, Leo Frobenius, and J.A. Rogers, among others.
    DT21.D8 1965
    LC-6516392

POLITICS-UNITED STATES

1. Carmichael, Stokeley. **Black Power: The Politics of Liberation in America**. New York, NY: Random House, 1967.

   This study represents a political framework and ideology to serve as an opportunity to resolve racial problems *"short of prolonged destructive guerilla warfare."* The study recommends that black people create their own political organizations to outline the demands and produce the kind of results needed to bring about social change. It includes an index, a bibliography and a note about Carmichael and co-author Charles V. Hamilton.

2. Hacker, Andrew. **Two Nations: Black and White, Separate, Hostile, Unequal**. New York, NY: Ballantine Books, 1995.

   An analytical study of racial segregation in America before and after legal segregation was struck down in 1955. Twelve chapters, three parts, references, acknowledgements, statistical sources, tables and an index are included.

   E185.615
   0345405374

3. Marable, Manning. **Race, Reform, and Rebellion: The Second Reconstruction in Black America, 1945-1990.** Jackson, MS: University Press of Mississippi, 1991.

   This book analyzes the status of black people in America since post-WWII to the end of the Reagan Administration. The author brings attention to the deterioration of the black working class and low-income communities since 1980 brought on by "deliberate federal and corporate policy." A chronicle of the influential organizations such as the Student Non-Violent Coordinating Committee (SNCC), the Black Panther Party (BPP), the League of Revolutionary Black Workers, and the Republic of New Afrika (NAPO) are also included. The increase of crack cocaine, violence, homelessness and imprisonment are closely examined for links to racial oppressive public policy reminiscent of the first Reconstruction following the Civil War. Chapter notes, bibliographical essay, a select bibliography, and an index included.

   E185.61.M352 1991
   0878054936

4. McCartney, John T. **Black Power Ideologies: An Essay in African-American Political Thought**. Philadelphia, PA: Temple University Press, 1992.

   This chronology of the history of black power begins with a background as to why black power is necessary. Subsequent chapters deal with black nationalist thought in the eighteenth and nineteenth-centuries, the Abolitionist movement, the influence of Booker T. Washington, Marcus Garvey, and Martin Luther King. The final chapters contain analysis of the influences of other key black leaders: Huey P. Newton, Shirley Chisholm, Elijah Muhammad, as well as an overall critical assessment of black power ideologies. Notes are included.

   E185.615.M334 192
   1566391458

5. Weiss, Nancy J. **Farewell to the Party of Lincoln: Black Politics in the Age of FDR**. Princeton, NJ: Princeton University Press, 1983.

   This work is a study in twelve chapters of the black political attitudes of the 1920s and '30s. Special emphasis is given to the black political behavior illustrated by black support of Roosevelt's New Deal in spite of poor support given racial issues. It includes illustrations, tables, a prologue, a conclusion, an appendix, a note on sources, and an index.

   E807.W44 1883
   0691047030

POLITICS-UNITED STATES, BLACK NATIONALISM

1. Delany, Martin. **Blake: or The Huts of America**. Boston, MA: Beacon Press, 1970.
   This political novel, originally written in 1861, introduces a political ideology that has come to be known as Black Nationalism. Delany is recognized by some as the "Father of Black Nationalism" as the result of this work.

2. Essien-Udom, Essien Udosen. **Black Nationalism: The Search for an Identity in America**. Chicago, IL: University of Chicago Press, 1962.
   This work examines the phenomenon of Black Nationalism in the United States—the effort of thousands of black people to resolve themselves of this fundamental problem of identity and to provide a context for their moral, cultural, and material advancement within the limits set by the American scene. The book describes the ideology of Black Nationalism, its organizations, leaders, and programs, focusing on the Nation of Islam—a Muslim movement led by Elijah (Poole) Muhammad.
   E185.61
   0226218538

3. Pinkney, Alphonso. **Red, Black and Green: Black Nationalism in the United States**. New York, NY: Cambridge University Press, 1976.
   This work offers a broad historical overview, general description, and analysis of Black Nationalism in the United States during 1963-1973 a period defined by the author as being the peak years of Black Nationalism. There are ten chapters that chronicle the development of Black Nationalism from early devotees such as Paul Cuffee, Martin Delany and Henry MacNeal Turner. The influences of Malcolm X, the Black Panther Party, cultural nationalism, religious nationalism, and educational nationalism are also examined. An epilogue, notes and an index are included.
   E185.615 .P54 1976
   052120887

4. Moses, Wilson J. **Classical Black Nationalism: From the American Revolution to Marcus Garvey**. New York, NY: University Press, 1996.
   This study chronicles the development of Black Nationalism from its development during the American colonial period to its revival occurring between 1895-1925. Each chapter offers primary source documents that fueled its development in America. Some of the unique offerings include *The Ethiopian Manifesto* (1829), David Walker's *Appeal*, Edward Wilmot Blyden's *"A Call of Providence to the Descendents of Africa in America*," and Marcus Garvey's address at Newport News in 1919.

PSYCHOLOGY

1. Akbar, Na'im. **Chains and Images of Psychological Slavery**. Jersey City, NJ: New Mind Productions, 1984.
   A collection of two essays that focus on the impact of slavery and the influences of Caucasian images for worship on the psychology of African-Americans. The author maintains that the African-Americans today still suffer from a Post-Traumatic Syndrome resulting from the experiences of chattel slavery. The first essay identifies certain characteristics that are illustrative of the kind of connection, which exists between the historical realities of slavery and the contemporary, social, and psychological characteristics of African-American communities. The second essay deals with the influence of racial religious imagery on the psychology of a people.
   E185.625.A44 1984
   093382100X

2. Fanon, Frantz. **Black Skin, White Masks**. New York, NY: Grove Press, 1967.

> This book is a classic examination of the African psyche by the prominent black French-Caribbean psychiatrist. This series of essays deals with the psychological damage inflicted upon Africans as the result of colonization and the constant message of white supremacy as reflected in the literature, and culture of French colonial societies. The author writes that in European societies "black" is associated with death, famine, sin, evil and wretchedness while "white" is viewed as "superior" and "desirable." The author points out that to the European, the African symbolizes the "*lower emotions, the base inclinations and the dark side of the soul.*" Fanon adds that the African acceptance of European culture is tantamount to the acceptance of African inferiority because at the core of the "*collective unconsciousness*" of European culture is the belief that the African is inferior.
>
> GN645.F313 1967
> LC67-30411

3. Grier, William H. **Black Rage**. New York, NY: Basic Books, 1968.

> A stern look at the racial attitudes and interactions of blacks and whites in America. This study asserts that the root of racism is the white historical perception of blacks as inferior. Racism is an American tradition and the rejection of this tradition by African-Americans is the subject of case studies examined. No index included.
>
> E185.625 .G68 1992
> 0465007015

4. Guthrie, Robert V. **Even the Rat Was White: A Historical View of Psychology**. Boston, MA: Allyn and Bacon, 1997.

> This is the second edition of a study designed to "*promote the use of non-traditional sources of documentation for the purpose of presenting, documenting and analyzing vignettes meaningful to the study of psychology from a non-traditional perspective.*" The work contains extensive research regarding blacks in the field of psychology and anthropology. Organized into nine chapters, the study also provides discussions of race and science, the U.S. census classification of black Americans and the history of the development of the Department of Psychology at Howard University. Included in the appendix are the 1938 U.S. miscegenation laws and a statement on racial psychology by the Society for the Psychological Study of Social Issues.
>
> BF105.G87 1997
> 0205149936

5. Jones, Reginald L. **Black Psychology**. Berkeley, CA: Cobb & Henry Publishers, 1991.

> This book is a classic collection of essays by black psychologists who advocate the creation of a discipline of psychology for the mental health treatment of black people in America. It includes Joseph L. White's classic essay "Toward a Black Psychology," where he asserts that traditional theories and treatments, when applied to black people, usually result in incorrect and condescending conclusions regarding the intelligence and cultural makeup of black America. Other contributors include: Na'im Akbar, Vernessa R. Clark, Wade Nobles, James P. Comer, Courtland C. Lee, Barbara J. Shade, Robert L. Williams, V.P. Franklin, James M. Jones, Joseph A. Baldwin, Lawrence E. Gary, Gayle D. Weaver, and others. Subject and author indexes are included.
>
> E 185.625 J66 1991
> 0943539056

7. Kardiner, Abram. **The Mark of Oppression: Explorations in the Personality of the American Negro**. New York, NY: World Publishing, 1962.

> This book is a re-issue of a controversial study of the black personality first published in 1951. The findings were debated and rejected by the nonscientific community largely on emotional grounds because they were *"too painful to accept."* Others in the psychology profession raised methodological objections related to the size of the sampling. Co-author is Lionel Ovesey.
>
> E185.625.K3 1962
> 0592019035

8. Wilson, Amos N. **The Developmental Psychology of the Black Child**. New York, NY: Africana Research Publishers, 1978.

> This study is aimed at practicing professionals in psychology and concerned others who wish to understand and help the black child. The author, a skilled psychologist and social activist, attempts to empower the helping profession to meet the challenges faced by African-Americans in order that they may assist black children.
>
> E185.86 W565 1978a
> OCLC5291999

RECONSTRUCTION-UNITED STATES, 1865-1877

1. Bentley, George R. **A History of the Freedman's Bureau**. Philadelphia, PA: University of Pennsylvania, 1955.

> This book presents a thorough treatment of the Freedman's Bureau with an examination of the status of blacks between slavery and emancipation. Analyses of major personalities, leaders, and their motives are included along with a critique of the programs fostered by the Bureau to assist blacks in making the transition from chattel to citizen. An index, a bibliography, an appendix and extensive notes are included.
>
> E185.2 B4
> LC55-9469

2. Du Bois, W.E.B. **Black Reconstruction in America, 1860-1880**. New York, NY: Russell & Russell, 1935.

> This book is a detailed study by a prominent sociologist using secondary resources to interpret the experience of black people during the first twenty years following reconstruction in America. Exhaustive and highly documented, this analysis reveals the U.S. government's betrayal and neglect of the needs of black people upon their release from chattel slavery. A bibliography and an index are provided.
>
> E668D83 1935
> OCLC317424

3. Logan, Rayford W. **Betrayal of the Negro: From Rutherford B. Hayes to Woodrow Wilson**. New York, NY: Collier Books, 1965.

> Originally published as *The Negro in American Life and Thought: The Nadir 1877-1901*, this book deals with the problems of black people and their place in America after the end of the Civil War and chattel slavery. An exhaustive examination of the status of the black man during the forty years following the end of the reconstruction period to the end of World War I, it chronicles the development of legal segregation and the second-class status of black people.
>
> E185.61.L64 1965
> LC65-23835

4. Lynch, John Roy. **The Facts of Reconstruction**. New York, NY: Arno Press, 1968.

> Lynch, who was a former Mississippi Congressman who served in the Mississippi State Senate from 1872-1875, wrote this book in defense of the reconstruction legislation. It is a primary source that provides insight into the political activities surrounding reconstruction in Mississippi and other parts of the South. Semi-autobiographical, Lynch does much to counter the "*rising tide of historical criticism*" between the years of 1900-1930.
>
> > E668.L98 1968
> > LC68-29009

RELIGION-AFRICA

1. Anderson, David A. **The Origin of Life on Earth: An African Creation Myth**. Mt. Airy, MD: Sights Production, 1991.

> This work retells the Yoruba creation myth in which the deity "Obatala" or "Lisa" descends from the sky to create the world. This work is a basic introduction into the cosmology of the Yoruba religion of West Africa.
>
> > PZ8.1.A543 Or 1991
> > 0962997854

2. Ben-Jochannan, Yosef. **African Origins of the Major Western Religions**. New York, NY: Alkebu-lan Books, 1970.

> This study traces the origins of the three major European religions: Christianity, Islam and Judaism to their African and Asian roots. Judaism, Christianity and Islam are referred to as the "*daughter, granddaughter, and great-granddaughter of the African God 'RA'.*" This work includes an extensive bibliography and chapter notes.
>
> > BL2400.B43
> > LC75-22630

3. Drake, St. Clair. **The Redemption of Africa and Black Religion**. Chicago, IL: Third World Press, 1970.

> The author examines the growth and development of black religion in the United States and the Caribbean and its vital role in the liberation movement toward "*freedom, identity and self-determination.*" The author introduces a concept of "*Ethiopianism*" which refers to a mode of thinking similar to the concept of "*Afrocentricity.*"
>
> > BR563.N4 D7
> > 0883780178

4. Mbiti, John S. **African Religions and Philosophy**. New York, NY: Heinemann, 1969.

> This is a collection of lectures delivered by the author during his days as a professor in Uganda and Germany. This work deals exclusively with traditional concepts and practices in African societies, which have not been studied in any systematic way before the colonial period. Mbiti writes that even the most educated and "*Europeanized*" African still holds many traditional African beliefs and practices that are rooted in his or her very being. A bibliography is included.
>
> > BL2400.M38 1969
> > LC70-76092

5. Paris, Peter, J. **The Spirituality of African Peoples: The Search for a Common Moral Discourse**. Minneapolis, MN: Fortress Press, 1994.

    This book is an interesting examination of the African cultural and moral foundations that support and define African spiritual life. The author uses "model comparative cultural analysis" to dissect the elements of African spiritual and cultural life. Index and bibliography included.

        BR563.N4 P38

        0800628543

RELIGION-CARIBBEAN

1. Barrett, Leonard E. **The Rastafarians**. Boston, MA: Beacon Press, 1988.

    This work is a historical examination of the Rastafarians and their link to the maroon societies of Africans who resisted slave life and started new nations in the hills of Jamaica. Chapter notes and bibliography provided.

        BL2532.R37 B37 1988

        080701027

RELIGION-UNITED STATES

1. Andrews, William. **Sisters of the Spirit: Three Black Women's Autobiographies of the Nineteenth Century.** Bloomington, IN: Indiana University Press, 1986.

    This book contains the previously published life stories of three black women spiritual leaders of early America: Jarena Lee, Zilpha Elaw, and Julia A.J. Foote. These women write of their "call" to Christian ministry during a time when gender prejudices against women ministers within the Church and in society, generally, were quite strong. These women are considered forerunners of the black female activist tradition found in the African-American Church and community.

        BV3780.S57 1986

        0253352606

3. Cone, James. **A Black Theology of Liberation**. Philadelphia, PA: Lippincott, 1970.

    The author writes that Christian theology is about liberation of the oppressed and that "*God is known to be where human suffering and humiliation prevails.*" Therefore, the author concludes that for black believers, Christian theology is one of liberation from racism. Index provided.

        BT78.C59 1970

        LC74-120333

4. Frazier, E. Franklin. **The Negro Church in America**. New York, NY: Schocken Books, 1963.

    This work presents a history of the development of the African-American Church in America from the enslavement period to the 1960s. Special attention is given to the development of the black church in its role as a social institution and as a model for the creation of mutual aid societies and insurance companies. The author notes the significant role of the Church in the everyday lives of black people was due to the restricted participation of black people in general American society. Included in this work are lyrics to early spirituals, a conclusion and an index.

        BR563.N4 F4 1963a

        LC62-19390

5. Johnson, Clifford H. **God Struck Me Dead: Voices of Ex-Slaves**. Cleveland, OH: Pilgrim's Press, 1993.

> Originally published in 1969, these original words from African slaves were found in an unpublished master's thesis at Fisk University. Their value today is quite important as it provides firsthand accounts of the religious life of slaves. These narratives were collected under the guidance of anthropologist, Paul Radin, who was a Fisk professor at the time. This project, under the direction of Charles S. Johnson at Fisk, served as a model for the Federal Writers Project of the Works Progress Administration of the 1930s.
> BV4930 G59 1993
> 0829809457

6. Lincoln, C. Eric. **The Black Church in the African-American Experience**. Durham, NC: Duke University Press, 1990.

> This ten-year study has examined the seven "mainline" denominations of the black religious community. The authors examine church relationships to politics, economics, women, youth, and music. Statistical tables, notes, bibliography, appendix and index are included. Co-Author is Lawrence H. Mamiya.
> BR563.N4 L55 1990
> 0822310732

7. Raboteau, Albert. **Slave Religion: The "Invisible Institution" in the Antebellum South**. New York, NY: Oxford University Press, 1978.

> Regarded as the "invisible institution" under slavery, the author provides a history of the religion of slaves from records left by slaves and former slaves. The author uses slave narratives, biographies, as well as travel accounts, missionary reports and journals of white observers to uncover elements that made up the slave religion. The author acknowledges and refers to the early research of John Blassingame, Sterling Stuckey, Eugene Genovese and others in this area. This work includes bibliographic notes and an index.
> BR563.N4 R25
> 0195024389

8. Wilmore, Gayraud S. **Black Theology: A Documentary History 1966-1979**. Maryknoll, NY: Orbis Books, 1994.

> This work is a compilation of "*significant documents of the Black Church and church-related movements to present the origin and development of Black Theology.*" Presented in four parts, this work examines theology in light of the Civil Rights and Black Power Movements. This work contains statements issued by the National Committee of Negro Churchmen concerning: "Black Power," "Independence Day," and the "Black Manifesto." Included are Vincent Harding's "Black Power and the American Christ"; Jacquelyn Grant's "Black Theology and the Black Woman"; James H. Cone's "The White Church and Black Power"; Cornel West's "Black Theology and Marxist Thought"; John Mbiti's "African Views American Black Theology"; Desmond Tutu's "Black Theology/African Theology Soul-Mates or Antagonists" and others.
> BT82.7B56
> 0883440415

SCIENCE-UNITED STATES

1. Finch, Charles S., III. **African Origins of Medical Science**. London, UK: Karnak House, 1990.

> This collection of essays examines ancient Egyptian medical traditions. This work represents a new historiography shedding light on the significant role of African cultural traditions in medical sciences. Other essays included are "Imhotep the Physician: Archetype of the Great Man," and "Science and Symbol in Egyptian Medicine," among others. Illustrations and notes are included.
> GN281 .F5 1991
> 0907015433

2. Van Sertima, Ivan. **Blacks in Science: Ancient and Modern**. New Brunswick, NJ: Transaction Books, 1983.

   This work is a serious treatment of models of African science paradigm outside of Ancient Egypt. Traditional approaches to science and technology among the Dogon of Mali, the ancient Kenyans, Nubians and other early Africans is examined in detail. The author points out that a recent finding in anthropology, archeology and related sciences may be credited with the rediscovery of the lost sciences of Africa while "*exploring the simplicities of tribal communities rather than the complexities found in the primary centers of large African nations.*"

   DT14. Q127.A4
   0878559418

SLAVE TRADE

1. Clarke, John Henrik. **Slave Trade and Slavery**. New York, NY: Holt, Rinehart and Winston, 1970.

   This is the second book in the Black Heritage series written for the general reader of history. It is a collection of essays by black history experts who dedicated their craft to creating black studies materials for educating Americans at all school levels and age groups.

   E441.S6
   030841542

2. Davidson, Basil. **The African Slave Trade**. Boston, MA: Back Bay Books, 1980.

   This book examines the nature of European-African relations in pre-colonial times. European merchants sold Africans into slavery in Europe, Brazil, the Caribbean, and the Americas as early as 1530. The author provides a chronology of the development of the slave trade and analyses of European ideas about Africa. The impact of slave trading upon Africa as a result of contact with Europe, and the growth of the trade is also discussed. A historical overview of old African states and English vessels are included along with a reading guide for additional study. Chapters are framed with quotes from European and Islamic scholars to set the theme of each of the seven parts. This work also has a variety of maps, a bibliography and an index.

   DT476.D32
   0316174386

3. Du Bois, W.E.B. **The Suppression of the African Slave Trade to the United States**. Williamstown, MA: Corner House Publishers, 1970.

   This early scientific study of the enslavement of African people in the United States was published in 1896 as a dissertation. It is the first of many significant contributions to black studies by the prolific author. This work examines the rise of the English Slave Trade in the planting, farming, and trading colonies of North America. It includes extensive data on each state regarding the spread and growth of slavery in every region, the debate on the status of Africans during the Revolutionary Period, 1774-1787, the role of the Spanish in the slave trade during the war between the US and England, the role of New York financial institutions in the "buying and selling" of Africans, and many other little known characteristics of slave trading in the United States. The appendices include: chronology of conspectus of colonial and state legislation restricting the African slave trade, 1641-1787, a chronology of state, national, and international legislation, 1788-1871, typical cases of vessels engaged in the American slave trade 1619-1864, a bibliography and an index.

   E441.D81 1970
   LC70-136148

4. Mannix, Daniel. **Black Cargoes: A History of the Trans Atlantic Slave Trade, 1518-1865**. New York, NY: Viking Press, 1962.

> A historical study of the Atlantic slave trade in twelve chapters exhibiting detailed research regarding the targets of this trade in human flesh. The author notes that slavers targeted children and young adults; "boys weighing 50 lbs sold for $500" which he notes represents a 30% increase over previous years. A chronology of "slave catching" by the Arabians on the Indian Ocean is also provided. An annotated bibliography, illustrations and index are included.
>
> > HT1049.M2
> > 0670001740

SLAVERY-AMERICAS

1. Thompson, Vincent B. **The Making of the African Diaspora in the Americas, 1441-1900**. New York, NY: Longmans, 1987.

> This book is a history of the dispersion of Africans to the Americas. The author, a professor in both the United States and Africa, begins with a description of slave societies in the Americas. The wealth and power aspects of these societies, as well as resistance in Africa to the passage to the Americas, are described. The rest of the book deals with the conflict that resulted from the strategy of the slavocracy and the strategy of the enslaved Africans in resistance to lifetime servitude. Appendices and a bibliography are included.
>
> > HT1048
> > 0582642388

SLAVERY-CARIBBEAN

1. Bush, Barbara. **Slave Women in Caribbean Society, 1650-1838**. London, UK: Heinemann, 1990.

> A scholarly study of the life and status of black slave women in Jamaica in an attempt to understand the historical dimensions of social and economic issues facing Jamaican women in contemporary society. Illustrations, maps and index included.
>
> > HT869.P6
> > 0852550588

SLAVERY-INSURRECTIONS

1. Aptheker, Herbert. **American Negro Slave Revolts**. New York, NY: International Publishers, 1993.

> Originally published in 1943, this is a chronology of slave revolts in the United States from 1791 through the end of the Civil War. The author illustrates in "*realistic terms the response of the American Negro to his bondage. The data herein presented to make necessary the revision of the generally accepted notion that his response was one of passivity and docility.*" A conclusion, an extensive bibliography and an index are included.
>
> > E447.A67 1993
> > 0717806057

2. Aptheker, Herbert. **Nat Turner's Slave Rebellion**. New York, NY: Grove Press, 1966.

> Originally a thesis for a Master's degree earned by the author at Columbia University in 1937, this work represents the first full-length study of Nat Turner's insurrection in Virginia. It also provides an examination of Virginian society, abolitionism, slavery and the condition leading up to the insurrection on August 21 and 22, 1831. List of persons murdered, list of black persons brought before the Southampton Court with owner's name, sentence, and bibliography are included.
>
> > F232.S7 A8 1966
> > OCLC20545175

3. Campbell, Mavis C. **The Maroons of Jamaica 1655-1796: A History of Resistance, Collaboration and Betrayal**. Trenton, NJ: African World Press, 1990.

> This book is a systematic study of African resistance to slavery in Jamaica and its integral role in the development of Maroon societies and its effect on Jamaican society in general. This book is produced from interviews with Maroon elders and descendants, old maps and other documents. The author lived with a group of Maroons in an attempt to improve her understanding of the Maroons. Jamaica was the first stop for most enslaved Africans. In Jamaica and other parts of the Caribbean, Africans were "prepared" or "seasoned" for life of enslavement through torture and abuse. Resistance is a natural path and some escaped to live in the hills. They fled and established new "habitation" away from plantations to the dismay of planters. These Maroon societies were symbols of resistance and rejection of a slave life. Planters hated and feared the Maroons and lived in danger of their wrath, particularly during 1720 through 1738. Some Maroon groups claim descent from the Arawak and Miskito Indians. Bibliography and index are included.
>
> F1884.C36 1990
> 0865430969

4. Egerton, Douglas R. **Gabriel's Rebellion: The Virginia Slave Conspiracies of 1800 and 1802**. Chapel Hill, NC: University of North Carolina Press, 1993.

> This book gives a history of the life of Gabriel Prosser, leader of slave rebellion in Virginia. The author researches the life of Prosser to "rescue" him from the myths and historical misinformation provided over the years. *"The book is a product of research conducted in ten repositories spread across five states and the District of Columbia, the fundamental source was the voluminous trial records stored in the Virginia State Library in Richmond."*
>
> F230.E37 1993
> 0807821136

5. James, C.L.R. **The Black Jacobins: Toussaint L'Ouverture and the San Domingo Revolution**. New York, NY: Vintage Books, 1963.

> This book is a detailed chronology of the only successful slave revolt in the western hemisphere where the hundreds of enslaved Africans organized under Toussaint L'Ouverture, a former slave, defeat the *"most powerful European powers of the day."* An extensive treatment of L'Ouverture is also included. The author refers to L'Ouverture as *"one of the most remarkable men of a period rich in remarkable men."*
>
> F1923.T85 1963
> 394702425

6. Katz, Jonathan. **Resistance at Christiana: The Fugitive Slave Rebellion, Christiana, Pennsylvania**. New York, NY: Thomas Y. Crowell, 1974.

> Like the John Brown Raid, the incident at Christiana, Pennsylvania on September 11, 1851, is considered to be a harbinger of the Civil War. The harsh U.S. fugitive slave law one year before was the cause of this rebellion where William Parker, a fugitive, led an armed gunfight against a federal marshal, a Maryland slaveholder and a posse who had come to recapture him and other runaway slaves hidden in the house. The incident is told using legal documents, court transcripts, archival collections and letters. It follows the life of William Parker to his successful escape and resettlement in Chatham, Canada. This work includes illustrations, chapter notes, a bibliography, and an index.
>
> E450K28 1974
> 0690003072

7. Katz, William Loren. **Breaking the Chains: African-American Slave Resistance**. New York, NY: Macmillan, 1990.

> This book is a history of resistance against slavery by those who were enslaved in America. This book addresses the stereotype that blacks were content with slavery and eventually gained "freedom" through the efforts of others by providing evidence of legal battles, work slowdowns, runaways, slave ship and plantation revolts by black people refusing to submit to forced labor in the New World. There is an interesting section examining music and lyrics as weapons of resistance. This work consists of thirteen chapters arranged into four parts: *Fighting Bondage on Land and Sea*; *Daily Toil, Perilous Struggle*; *Flight and Revolt*, and *Marching to Freedom*. A bibliography and index are included.
>> E447.K38 1990
>> 0689314930

8. Price, Richard. **Maroon Societies: Rebel Slave Communities in the Americas**. Baltimore, MD: Johns Hopkins University, 1979.

> This study of the free communities established by escaped slaves in the Caribbean, Latin America and the United States, explores maroon societies in each region of the "New World" and provides excerpts from historical and contemporary scholars such as Capitan Stedman, who fought for five years to free blacks in Surinam, Yvan Debbasch, a French scholar who writes of the maroon community of Le Maniel in Haiti, and Silvia W. De Groot, chronicler of the *Bush Negroes of Surinam*. It includes bibliographical notes and an index.
>> HT1048.P74 1979
>> 9780801854965

SLAVERY-SOUTH AMERICA

1. Degler, Carl N. **Neither Black Nor White: Slavery and Race Relations in Brazil and the United States**. New York, NY: Macmillan Publishing Company, 1971.

> This examination of black-white relationships in the U.S. and Brazil aims to explain the differences in the contemporary racial patterns of both countries. The author notes differences such as the racial status of mulattoes in each country, the legacy of slavery in both countries and why Brazil did not develop a racial defense of African slavery like the antebellum South.
>> F2659.N4 D42
>> LC73-130946

2. Freyre, Gilberto. **The Masters and the Slaves: A Study in the Development of Brazilian Civilization**. New York, NY: Knopf, 1956.

> Translated from Portuguese by Samuel Putnam, this is an anthropological study in the development of Brazilian civilization. Originally published in 1946, this book examines the characteristics of Portuguese colonization of Brazil into an "agrarian, slave-holding and hybrid society" with a distinctive color caste system that favors light skin tones over dark skin tones. This work is arranged into five chapters dealing with general characteristics of Portuguese colonization, Portuguese relations with the Incas, Mayans, and Aztecs, an examination of the Portuguese as "colonizer" and the slave life in Brazil. A glossary and a biography of the author are included. This edition is revised and abridged from the second English-Language edition. Glossary is included.
>> F2510.F75243
>> 0394301943

SLAVERY-UNITED STATES

1. Blassingame, John W. **The Slave Community: Plantation Life in the Antebellum South**.
New York, NY: Oxford University Press, 1979.
   This is an analytical description of the life of a *"black slave: his African heritage, culture, family, acculturation, behavior, religion, and personality."* The significance of this work is the scholar's use of personal records left by the slave and other nontraditional sources. The author writes, *"a great deal of emphasis has been placed on non-traditional sources, such as black autobiographies examined in light of traditional historical records."* Organized in seven chapters, the author has also provided an appendix with Critical Essays on Sources, a Comparative Examination of Total Institutions and a select bibliography.
   E443.B55
   0195025636

2. Dumond, Dwight. **Antislavery: The Crusade for Freedom in America**. Ann Arbor, MI: The University of Michigan Press, 1961.
   The author describes this study as *"the story of the classic contest between slavery and freedom in America. Slavery was the complete subjection by force of one person to the will of another, recognized and sustained by state law. The contest between slavery and the foundation principles of democracy began in the early eighteenth century and continues to the present time. The course of the men and women who dedicated their lives to arresting the spread of slavery was marvelously directed and straightforward. They denounced it as a sin that could only be remedied by unconditional repentance and retributive justice. These people were neither fanatics nor incendiaries. They appealed to the minds and consciences of men."* Bibliography and index are included.
   E441.D84
   OCLC36335970

3. Gaspar, David Barry and Hine, Darlene Clark. **More Than Chattel: Black Women and Slavery in the Americas**. Bloomington, IN: Indiana University Press, 1996.
   This book is a collection of historical essays (all by women scholars) focusing on the status of black women during slavery. Stereotypes, myths and half-truths are all addressed effectively in this work while providing a thoughtful historical analysis on the experience of black women. Index and bibliography are included.
   HT1049.M62
   0253330173

4. Genovese, Eugene. **Roll, Jordan, Roll: The World the Slaves Made**. New York, NY: Vintage Books, 1976.
   This is a detailed history of the life of enslaved Africans in America. The author's approach is quite different as noted by his definition of enslaved blacks as a *"black nation"* who are responsible for laying the foundation for *"a separate black national culture"* that has greatly enriched the dominant white culture of America. In four parts, the author examines the lifestyle and culture of slaves in order to *"present it as accurately as possible."* Extensive chapter notes, a subject and name index, and a biography of the author are included.
   E443.G46 1976
   0394716523

5. Genovese, Eugene D. **The Political Economy of Slavery: Studies in the Economy and Society of the Slave South.** New York, NY: Random House, 1967.

> This book is comprised of several studies on the economy of the slave south. Presented in four sections, the author maintains that slavery produced in the south a "*social system and civilization with a distinct class structure, political community, economy, ideology and set of psychological patterns*" that were in conflict with the rest of the nation and the developing world. Slavery gave the south a small, yet powerful ruling white class and a regional social order, which was dominated by the slave labor system. This book is organized into four sections and ten chapters. In section one and two, the author provides an interpretation of the slave south, examines slave labor patterns, productivity rates, soil exhaustion and the limits of southern agricultural reform. Sections three and four deal with the economic significance of the plantation, industrialists under slavery, type of labor in southern factories and the origins of slavery expansionism. Included are notes, a bibliography, and an index.
>
>> E442.G45 1965
>> 394704002

6. Huggins, Nathan Irvin. **Black Odyssey: The African-American Ordeal in Slavery.** New York, NY: Vintage Books, 1979.

> This is a concise history of the life of enslaved Africans in America and an examination of how these Africans developed a culture that instilled in them a sense of meaning and coherence as a people in spite of their survival of two hundred or more years of servitude and subhuman legal status. The author provides an in-depth look at the psychological dynamics of slavery in social, cultural, and economic terms. This work consists of eight chapters, an epilogue and a bibliographical note.
>
>> E441.H89 1979
>> 0394726871

7. Johnson, Michael and Roark, James L. **Black Masters.** New York, NY: Norton, 1984.

> The history of a free man named William Ellison, a master craftsman who made cotton gins, is presented in this work. He represented a minority of free blacks who were economically independent and "*one of the wealthiest free persons of color in the South and wealthier than nine out of ten whites*" in antebellum South Carolina. Family letters were found under a house in 1935 and led eventually to this history of William Ellison's life and family experience in the antebellum South. Maps, illustrations, notes and an index are included.
>
>> F279.C49 N43 1984
>> 0393019063

8. Stampp, Kenneth M. **The Peculiar Institution: Slavery in the Ante-Bellum South.** New York, NY: Vintage Books, 1989.

> This classic work is a study of slavery in ten chapters to understand slavery and the effect it has on American society. The author states "*one must know what slavery meant to the Negro and how he reacted to it before one can comprehend his more recent tribulations.*" Stampp addresses myths about blacks and their "uniqueness" for bondage, the inhumanity of blacks as promoted by slavery proponents and white supremacists. This work includes a bibliography of manuscripts consulted and an index.
>
>> E441 .S8 1956
>> 394702530

9. Still, William. **The Underground Railroad**. New York, NY: Arno Press, 1968.

A reprint of the 1873 book of narratives, facts, letters chronicling the escape of enslaved blacks to freedom in northern states, Canada and Europe by William Still of the Philadelphia Anti-Slavery Society. It is a record of covert activities of runaway slaves and abolitionists to rid the country of slavery and influence public opinion against the business of human bondage. The editor, William Still, is a descendant of free blacks who purchased their freedom and farmed in New Jersey. Still moved to Philadelphia where he taught himself to read and write and joined the Philadelphia Vigilance Committee to "*offer aid and comfort to the slave runaways*." He was Chairman of the Pennsylvania Abolition Society by 1851. Illustrations are included.

    E450.S85 1968
    LC68-29019

10. Walker, David. **David Walker's Appeal in Four Articles: Together with a Preamble, to the Coloured Citizens of the World, But in Particular, and Very Expressly, to Those of the United States of America**. New York, NY: Hill and Wang, 1965.

Written in antebellum America, Walker's Appeal is a call to blacks to assume control of their lives and of a country where they are demoralized daily and dehumanized by the institution of slavery. Walker's Appeal and his efforts to "*circulate it among the slave population represents one of the boldest and innovative plans*" for black empowerment and resistance to the declaration of black inferiority and perpetual enslavement. Historian Charles M. Wiltse edits this work and provides an introduction.

    E446.W178 1965
    OCLC37703819

11. Wood, Peter. **Black Majority**. New York, NY: W.W. Norton & Company, 1974.

This work is a history of enslaved Africans in Colonial South Carolina from 1670 through the Stono Rebellion of 1739. It is an award-winning study of the black population during enslavement. The study is in four parts with chapters on the development of the Gullah language, patterns of resistance to slavery, and patterns of white control of enslaved Africans. Extensive appendices, a bibliography and index are included.

    E445.87 W66 1974
    0393007774

SOCIOLOGY-AFRICA

1. Fanon, Frantz. **The Wretched of the Earth: The Handbook of the Third World Revolution.**
New York, NY: Grove Press, Inc., 1963.

At the time of its original publication (1963), this book was regarded as a handbook of revolutionary thought and action inspired by the growth of independence movements in Africa and other "third world" areas. The author, psychiatrist and spokesman for the Algerian revolution, also examines the psyche of the colonized in a three-part section entitled: "*Colonial War and Mental Disorders.*" Fanon warns liberated people not to imitate their former oppressors but to create new solutions to problems their colonizers were not able or willing to resolve. Jean-Paul Sartre writes the preface. The work consists of five sections and a conclusion.

    DT33.F313 1963
    LC65-14196

SOCIOLOGY-AFRICA, WOMEN

1. Hay, Margaret Jean. **African Women South of the Sahara**. New York, NY: Longmans, 1985.
   This is a study of the African woman in the urban and traditional societies of Africa. Each chapter focuses on a select aspect of life and the role of women in three parts with an appendix, a bibliography, an index and notes on contributors. Part 1: Women in the Economy; Part 2: Women in Society and Culture; and Part 3: Women in Politics and Policy. Contributors are African studies specialists from American and African universities.
   HQ1788.A57 1985
   0582643732

SOCIOLOGY-CARIBBEAN

1. Acosta-Belen, Edna. **The Puerto Rican Woman: Perspectives on Culture, History, and Society**. New York, NY: Praeger Publishers, 1979.
   This history of women in Puerto Rico begins with an overview of the indigenous Taino Indian women during pre-Columbian times on the island. The strong tradition of male chauvinism in Puerto Rican culture attempts to dismiss feminism and ideas of women's liberation as divisive and foreign but this collection of works by Puerto Rican women scholars provides sound arguments for equality among women and men in Puerto Rico. This work consists of eleven chapters dealing with some aspect of women's life in Puerto Rico: History of Women's Movement; Feminism and its effect; the education and professional status of Puerto Rican women; the black Puerto Rican woman; the cultural response to female homosexuality and the ideology and images of women in contemporary Puerto Rico. This work puts emphasis on social conditions and the changing social role of women as a result of political activity and feminism.
   HQ1522.P83
   003524660

SOCIOLOGY-SOUTH AMERICA

1. de Jesus, Carolina Maria. **Child of the Dark: The Diary of Carolina Maria de Jesus**. New York, NY: New America Library, 1960.
   This is the journal of a black mother living in the slums of Sao Paulo, Brazil in the late 1950s. This journal, written in "*stark simplicity*," provides a look into the daily lives of a poor family and their environs in a large urban city in Brazil.
   F2631.J49
   LC62-14719

SOCIOLOGY-UNITED STATES

1. Allen, Theodore W. **The Invention of the White Race: Racial Oppression and Social Control (Invention of the White Race)**. New York, NY: Verso, 1994.
   This work, in two volumes, approaches racial slavery as a particular form of racial oppression, and racial oppression as a "*sociogenic*"—rather than a "phylogenic"—phenomenon, homologous with gender and class oppression. Also, in considering the phenomenon of racial slavery, the book focuses primarily not on why the bourgeoisie in continental Anglo-America had recourse to that anachronistic form of labor, slavery, but rather how they could establish and maintain for such a long historical period, that degree of social control without which no motive of profit or prejudice could have had effect. Bibliography and index are included.
   E185 .A44 1994
   0860914801

2. Bell, Derrick. **Faces at the Bottom of the Well: The Permanence of Racism**. New York, N.Y.: Basic Books, 1992.

> This work addresses the dynamics of racism in America and the inability of blacks to eliminate American society's long-held belief in the subordination of black people and the maintenance of the white power structure. Bell uses fiction and situational stories to argue the permanence of racism. Each tale depicts a possible situation that the African-American populous will have to confront. Bell, given current legislative practices and legal statute, critiques how each scenario can be manipulated or dismantled in order to maintain the status quo.
>
> > E185.615.B395 1992b
> > 0465068146

3. Cose, Ellis. **The Rage of a Privileged Class**. New York, NY: Harper Collins Publishers, 1993.

> This collection of personal encounters of institutional and personal racism experienced by upper class black Americans in the larger white society, this book provides modern-day examples to illustrate the continued existence of racism and racial prejudice in American society.
>
> > E 185.86 C5883 1993
> > 0060182696

4. Drake, St. Clair and Clayton, Horace R. **Black Metropolis: A Study of Negro Life in a Northern City**. New York, NY: Harcourt, Brace & World, Inc, 1945.

> This is a study of the growing black population of Chicago in an effort to provide a statistical base of data for providing analysis of social conditions for urban planning and providing services. Similar reports were undertaken through the United States as the urban population of blacks continued to increase and the economic activity diversified. The study is presented in two volumes. Extensive tables, charts, maps, an index and an appendix are included.
>
> > F548.9.N3 D8
> > LC57-5271

5. Du Bois, W. E. B. **The Souls of Black Folk: Essays and Sketches**. New York, NY: Penguin Books, 1989.

> Originally published in 1903, this examination of the history and psychology of black people in the United States has been in print continually. It is a scholarly and thoughtful review of the legacy and status of black people at the beginning of the twentieth century. Chapters one through two review Emancipation and its aftermath. Chapter three reviews the rise of personal leadership. Generally this work focuses on black life within "The Veil" and concludes with a chapter on African-American song and its social and spiritual significance.
>
> > E185.6.D797 1989
> > 014039074X

6. Higginbotham, Evelyn Brooks. **Righteous Discontent: The Women's Movement in the Black Baptist Church 1880-1920**. Cambridge, MA: Harvard University Press, 1993.

> In this study of the black woman in the Baptist church from 1880 to 1920, the author documents the role played by black women in *"broadening the public arm of the church and making it the most powerful institution of racial self-help in the African-American community."* An extensive index and bibliographic notes are included.
>
> > BX644.H54 1993
> > 0674769775

7. Jackson, George. **Soledad Brother: The Prison Letters of George Jackson**. New York, NY: Bantam Books, 1970.

    This narrative is written in the form of letters written by George Jackson while jailed in the California Soledad prison and published soon after his robbery conviction. Jackson's writings were translated in several languages and acclaimed throughout the world as the "*most powerful and eloquent black writer since Malcolm X.*" The extraordinary courage, integrity, and humanity of his letters led Jackson to become a symbol for the struggle of all oppressed people.

        HV9468.J3
        LC 77-139252

8. Lecky, Robert S. and Wright, H. Elliott. **Black Manifesto: Religion, Racism, and Reparations**. New York, NY: Sheed and Ward, 1969.

    This work is an investigation into the issues related to the black demand for reparations by James Foreman and the National Black Economic Development Conference (NBEDC) and its effect on the Christian Church and general American society in 1969. Contributors are: Robert Browne, Fairleigh Dickinson University; Harvey Cox, Harvard University; James Foreman, SNCC; Dick Gregory, activist/comedian; James Lawson, chair of the Black Methodists for Church Renewal in Memphis; Robert Lecky, United Methodist minister; Stephen C. Rose, author of the "Grass Roots Church"; William Strongfellow, attorney and theologian; and H. Elliott Wright, editor of religious news service. A chronology and a bibliography are included.

        E185.615 .L4
        836200806

9. West, Cornel. **Race Matters**. Boston, MA: Beacon Press, 1993.

    The author discusses the major issues that make race matter in contemporary American society. Issues discussed include: nihilism in black America; the pitfalls of racial reasoning; the crisis in black leadership; the new black conservatism; black equality and identity; black-Jewish relations; black sexuality and black rage.

        E185.615 W43 1993
        0807009180

10. Willis-Thomas, Deborah. **Picturing Us: African-American Identity in Photography**. New York, NY: New Press, 1994.

    This book contains a collection of photographs of Africans and African-Americans in four parts with text explaining the significance of the image as storyteller. Essays are from Vertamae Smart-Grosvenor, Bell Hooks, E. Ethelbert Miller, Robert Hill, Angela Davis, Adele Logan Alexander, Christian Walker and others.

        TR680
        1565841077

11. Wilson, William Julius. **The Declining Significance of Race: Blacks and Changing American Institutions**. Chicago, IL: University of Chicago Press, 1980.

    This is the second edition of a still controversial study regarding the role of race in discrimination in America. The author presents the argument that "class" as a factor is more important in the plight of the black underclass than "race" in America. The author examines racial oppression, economic class subordination, slavery, the plantation hegemony and other issues. The original 1978 bibliography is included along with a supplemental bibliography, notes and index.

        E185.W73 1980
        0226901297

12. Woodson, Carter G. **A Century of Negro Migration**. Washington, DC: Association for the Study of Negro Life and History, 1918.

> The author explains the purpose of this book as an attempt to *"present in succinct form the leading facts as to how the Negroes in the United States have struggled under adverse circumstances to flee from bondage and oppression in quest of a land offering asylum to the oppressed and opportunity to the fortunate."* This study was written at the beginning of the migration of black people from the rural southern towns to the urban centers of the United States. This work is composed of nine chapters, a bibliography, an index, maps and diagrams indicating the black population from 1900-1910.
>> E185.9
>> LC18-17856

SOCIOLOGY-UNITED STATES, FAMILY

1. Billingsley, Andrew. **Black Families in White America**. New York, NY: Simon & Schuster, Inc., 1988.

> This study examines how European American family norms have influenced African-American families. Organized into seven chapters that probe deeply to understand the issues, strengths and challenges of the black family, this book could serve as a handbook for policymakers, as well as social and health care professionals in caring for and understanding black families. It includes statistics, tables, figures, and preface to the original 1968 edition, a conclusion and index.
>> E185.86B5 1988
>> 0671671626

2. Frazier, E. Franklin. **The Negro Family in the United States**. New York, NY: Dryden Press, Inc., 1951.

> This is an examination of the black family and the effect of slavery upon the composition of the family and familial attitudes and behaviors. Issues of monogamy, polygamy, family structure and others are analyzed. An index, notes, and a bibliography are included.
>> E185.86 F74 1951
>> LC66-13868

3. Hare, Nathan and Hare, Julia. **The Endangered Black Family: Coping with the Unisexualization and the Coming Extinction of the Black Race**. San Francisco, CA: Black Think Tank, 1986.

> This work is an analysis of the challenges facing black families in America, beginning with the controversial Moynihan Report and similar research approaches taken by black psychologists and sociologists. The authors believe black social science researchers are ignoring the warning signs and *"pretend that all is well with the black family despite our recognized economic, educational and political deprivation."* A product of fifteen years of research, the authors point to the detrimental role played by feminism and homosexuality in the breakdown of the black family. This work is divided into three parts: *"The Deception," "The Blueprint and Program for Genocide,"* and *"The Reconstruction."* Notes, references and an index are included.
>> HQ755.5.U5 H37 1986
>> 0961308605

4. Hill, Robert B. **The Strength of Black Families**. New York, NY: Emerson Hall, 1972.
   The author contends that examining the "strengths of the black family can contribute as much toward the understanding and ameliorating of social problems as examining their weaknesses." This is a study of black families in six areas: (1) Strong kinship bonds; (2) Strong work orientation; (3) Adaptability of family roles; (4) High achievement orientation; (5) Religious orientation; and (6) summary, notes, and bibliography.
   E185.86 H66 1972
   0878290087

5. McAdoo, Harriette Pipes. **Black Families**. Thousand Oaks, CA: Sage Publications, 1997.
   This is a classic examination of the black family in five parts: Part I: Historical and theoretical conceptualizations of African-American families; Part II: Family patterns: economics and social mobility; Part III: Socialization within African-American families; Part IV: Gender relations within African-American communities; and Part V: Advocacy and family policies for African-American families. The essays are by noted professionals such as Wade W. Nobles, Robert B. Hill, John L. McAdoo and Marian Wright Edelman.
   E185.86
   0803955723

6. Nobles, Wade W. and Goddard, Lawford L. **African-American Families: Issues, Insights, and Directions**. Oakland, CA: Black Family Institute, 1987.
   This study of the African-American family is based on the theoretical model, "Africanity" developed by the Oakland-based Black Family Institute. This model of "Africanity" seeks to uncover and define the underlying "principles which determine the intrinsic nature or integrity" of black family life in order to "explicate and investigate enterprise that is consistent with African-American reality." This work highlights the Africanity model, which is sought and utilized due to the failure and inappropriateness of conventional family therapy methodology when applied to black families. A discussion and study guide, a glossary and an index are included.
   E185.86 A327 1987
   0939205041

7. Staples, Robert. **The Black Family: Essays and Studies**. Belmont, CA: Wadsworth Publishing Company, 1978.
   This work continues to be updated as it provides the undergraduate or general reader with an overview of research regarding the black family in the United States in four parts: "The Setting," a review of historical studies of the black family; "The Dyad," a look at black male/female relationships; "The Family," an examination of childrearing, parental roles, the extended family and personality development; "Black Families and the Future," a review of alternative lifestyles and public policy and their effect on the black family. Some contributors include Wade Nobles, Frances Beale, Alan P. Bell, Leanor Johnson, Delores Mack, Patricia Bell Scott, and others. A selected bibliography is included.
   E185.86.S7 1978
   0534005578

SOCIOLOGY-UNITED STATES, MEN

1. Madhubuti, Haki and Karenga, Maulana. **Million Man March/Day of Absence: A Commemorative Anthology**. Chicago, IL: Third World Press, 1996.

> This is a collection of poetry, essays, speeches, photographs and illustrations from the Million Man March of October 16, 1995. In addition to Madhubuti, the contributors include Maulana Karenga, Louis Farrakhan, Jesse L. Jackson, Cornel West, Selwyn Hinds, E. Ethelbert Miller, Mari Evans, Gwendolyn Brooks, Alice Walker, Tiamoyo Karenga, Courtney Horne and many others. Photographers and illustrators include: J.D. Howard, Robert Sengstacke, Tom Feelings, Murry DePillars and others.
>
> E185.86.M54 1996
> 0883781883

2. Madhubuti, Haki R. **Black Men: Obsolete, Single, Dangerous?: The Afrikan-American Family in Transition: Essays in Discovery, Solution and Hope**. Chicago, IL: Third World Press, 1990.

> The author responds to the perplexing questions: *"Black men: obsolete, single and dangerous?"* in a scholarly and insightful work of essays and poems, divided into three parts: (1) The Changing Seasons; (2) Mission and Visions; and (3) Worldview. The author analyzes contemporary black life with compassion and courage. He also offers strategies to ensure the survival and empowerment of the black family.
>
> E185.86.M33 1990
> 0883781352

3. Majors, Richard G. **The American Black Male: His Present Status and His Future**. Chicago, IL: Nelson-Hall Publishers, 1994.

> The book seeks to provide an understanding of the black male experience in America by presenting health, economic, and educational issues that affect black males. The author writes that young urban black males are often *"miseducated, mishandled, mislabeled and mistreated by society."* In addition, Majors point out that stereotypes about black men have caused deep fear in the general society resulting in the demonstration of abnormal behavior by black males toward society and life. Essays by a wide variety of professionals, such as co-author Jacob U. Gordon, Professor of Africana studies; William Brooks, GM Corporation Personnel Director; Fabricio Balcar, Psychologist; William Andrews, professor; Edith Freeman, Professor of Social Work; Billy Jones, MD, Mental Health Specialist; and Jewelle Taylor Gibbs, Ph.D., a specialist in adolescent psychology, to name a few.
>
> E185.86.A42
> 083041236

SOCIOLOGY-UNITED STATES, WOMEN

1. Collins, Patricia Hill. **Black Feminist Thought: Knowledge, Consciousness, and the Politics of Empowerment**. New York, NY: Routledge, 1991.

> This examination of the lives of black women in American society begins with a chapter analyzing personal experiences of the author noting the similarities faced by other black women: *"I tried to disappear into myself in order to deflect the painful, daily assaults designed to teach me that being an African-American, working-class woman made me lesser than those who were not."* The author views her work as a voice *"in the dialogue among people who had been silenced"* and an attempt to *"reconcile subjectivity and objectivity"* in scholarship. References, a note about the author, and an index are included.
>
> HQ1426.C633 1991
> 0415905974

2. Comas-Diaz, Lillian and Greene, Beverly. **Women of Color: Integrating Ethnic and Gender Identities in Psychotherapy**. New York, NY: Guilford Press, 1994.

   This unique collection of essays is related to the varied life experiences of women of color and different cultures and their unique therapeutic needs. Contributors provide suggestions of therapy that is successful with women of color. The contributors point out that the life experiences of these women differ from that of middle class white women because of racial prejudice and other secondary factors. In addition, the authors note that there is also a variety of life experiences within each cultural group based upon such factors as sexual orientation, age, social and economic status. Contributors include practicing psychiatrists, medical professionals, social workers, clinical psychologists, and university professors specializing in mental health, counseling psychology and ethnic studies.

   RC451.4.M58 W66 1994
   0898623715

3. St. Jean, Yanick and Feagin, Joe R. **Double Burden: Black Women and Everyday Racism**. Armonk, NY: M.E. Sharpe, 1998.

   This is an analytical collection of authentic experiences of black women in American society and their encounters with racism. The author also examines the status, perception and myths concerning black women in American society. This work offers an evaluative look at society from the black woman's perception and how society's perception of the black woman has affected the self-concept and self-esteem of black females generally. There are eight chapters: The Lives of Black Women; Black Women at Work; Black Beauty in a Whitewashed World; Common Myths and Media Images; Distancing White Women, Black Families, Motherhood and Families; and Finale. Notes and an index are included.

   E185.86.S695 1998
   1563249448

APPENDIX A - Department Survey 1998
African-American Studies Core List Project
Georgia State University – Atlanta

Department or Program Chair's instructions: Please answer each inquiry about your institution's African-American studies department or program, and return it with any other participant's survey, syllabi and/or reading lists using the enclosed postage-paid envelope to: M. Elaine Hughes, Information Services Department, Pullen Library, Georgia State University, Atlanta, GA 30303. For more information call 404-651-2185, email Akilah Nosakhere at libasn@gsu.edu or visit the project web page at http://www2.gsu.edu/~libmeh/corelist.html

Thank you for taking the time to complete this important survey!

1. In what year was the African-American studies department/program at your institution started? _____

2. Is your institution: _____public _____private

3. How many different African-American studies courses were offered last academic year?
    _____Number of undergraduate courses   _____ Number of undergraduate courses

4. List the most popular African-American studies courses among students on your campus:
    _____
    _____
    _____

5. Approximately how many of the African-American studies courses are cross-listed under other departments?
    _____

Please list the other departments that have African-American studies courses cross-listed:

_____
_____
_____

APPENDIX B - Participant Survey 1998
African-American Studies Core List Project
Georgia State University - Atlanta

Instructions: Please answer each inquiry as completely as possible and return syllabi and reading lists using the enclosed postage-paid label. Thank you for taking the time to complete this important survey.

1. Check the type of institution in which you currently teach: (check one)
    a. ___public institution   ___private institution
    b. Are graduate level degrees granted by your institution? ___Yes   ___No
    c. The academic term is:___quarter   ___semester

2. In what year was the African-American studies (A.A.S.) department/program at your institution started? _____ (optional)

3. Indicate the number of years you have taught A.A.S. courses at the college level:
    ___1-5 years   ___6-10 years   ___10-20 years ___20+

4. Sex: ___Female   ___Male

5. Age Range: ___25-35   ___36-45   ___46-55   ___56-65   ___65+

6. Highest Degree completed:
    a.   ___Ph.D.   ___Ed.D.   ___M.D.   ___M.S.   ___M.A.
         ___M.B.A. ___J.D.   ___B.A.   ___B.S.
         ___Other:_____
    b.   Please indicate your major area of study: _____

7. List all academic departments in which you teach classes:
    _____   _____

8. Which is your primary or "home" department?
    _____

9. List the most popular A.A.S. courses among students on your campus:
    _____
    _____

10. How many **different** African-American studies **courses** were offered last year?
    _____

11. What is the percentage of A.A.S. courses cross-listed under other departments?
    _____

12. What is the total number of students enrolled in **your** A.A.S. courses this term?
    _____

African-American Studies Core List Project 1998 - Page 2

13. Do you find it difficult to secure textbooks and other instructional resources in
    African-American studies?   ___No   ___Yes
    If yes, check all that apply: ___Out of print   ___Too expensive
                                       ___Not readily available, because:

    _____

    _____

14. List the subject areas in which you find it difficult to locate appropriate textbooks and
    instructional resources:

    _____

    _____

15. Please list each A.A.S. courses you currently teach. Indicate the Title(s) and /or
    Author(s) of the required textbook(s) used in each undergraduate or graduate course:
    (attach syllabi or continue on page 4)   Indicate level: U - undergraduate or G-
    graduate)   **Textbook Title:**

    _____   _____

    _____   _____

    _____   _____

16. Do you assemble special course packets or readings for instructional use?
    ___No ___Yes

17. If Yes, please rank the top five (5) resources (books, maps, films, electronic files, etc.)
    used as optional or enrichment materials in each of the courses you teach:

    (1-most important, 5-least important)

	Undergraduate courses	Graduate courses
1.	_____	_____
2.	_____	_____
3.	_____	_____
4	_____	_____
5.	_____	_____

18. How frequently do you electronically access or physically use your institution's library to
    prepare for instruction of A.A.S. Courses?
    ___Frequently ___Occasionally   ___Rarely   ___Never

19. Do you find that your library has the majority of items needed for instruction in African-
    American studies courses?   ___No ___Yes

20. Additional Comments or Clarifications:

Thank you for completing this survey. Please return it promptly with your comments, copies of
course syllabi, and optional readings lists, using the postage-paid label provided.

APPENDIX C - Years of Teaching African American Studies

Survey Question 6: *Indicate the number of years you have taught African American Studies courses at the college/university level*

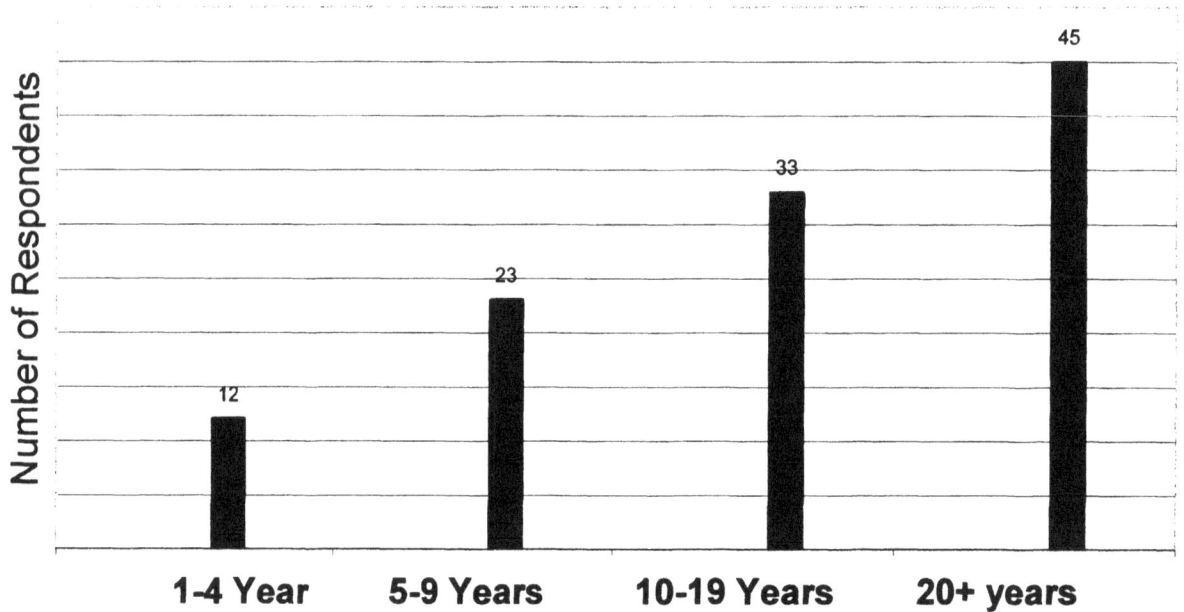

Total Number of Respondents: 113

APPENDIX D - Educational Background

Survey Question 7: *What is the highest degree you have competed?*

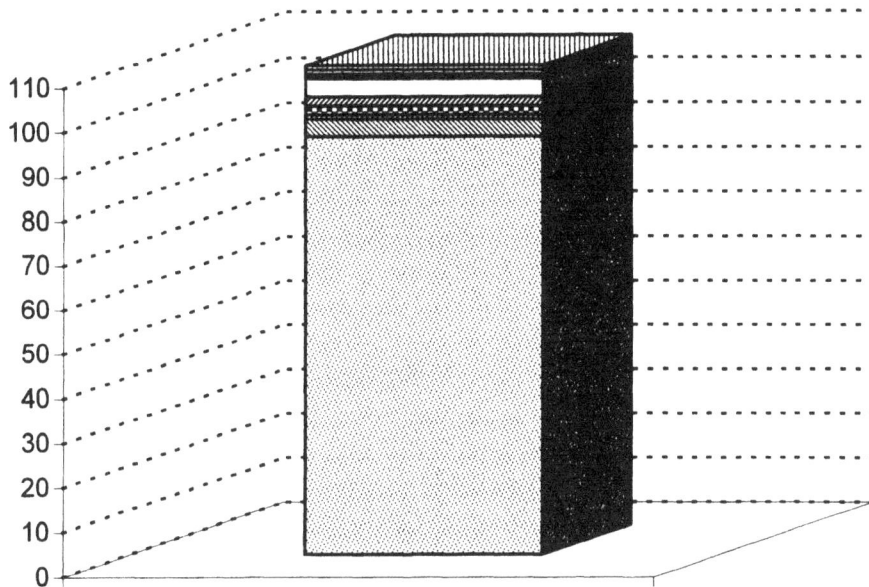

94	4	1	2	2	4	1	1	1
■Ph.D.	▨Ed.D.	▨M.D.	▧J.D.	▨M.S.	□M.A.	■B.A.	▢B.S.	□B.F.A.

Total Number of Respondents: 110

APPENDIX E - Top Three Administrative Homes
Survey Question 12: *What is your tenure granting department or administrative home?*

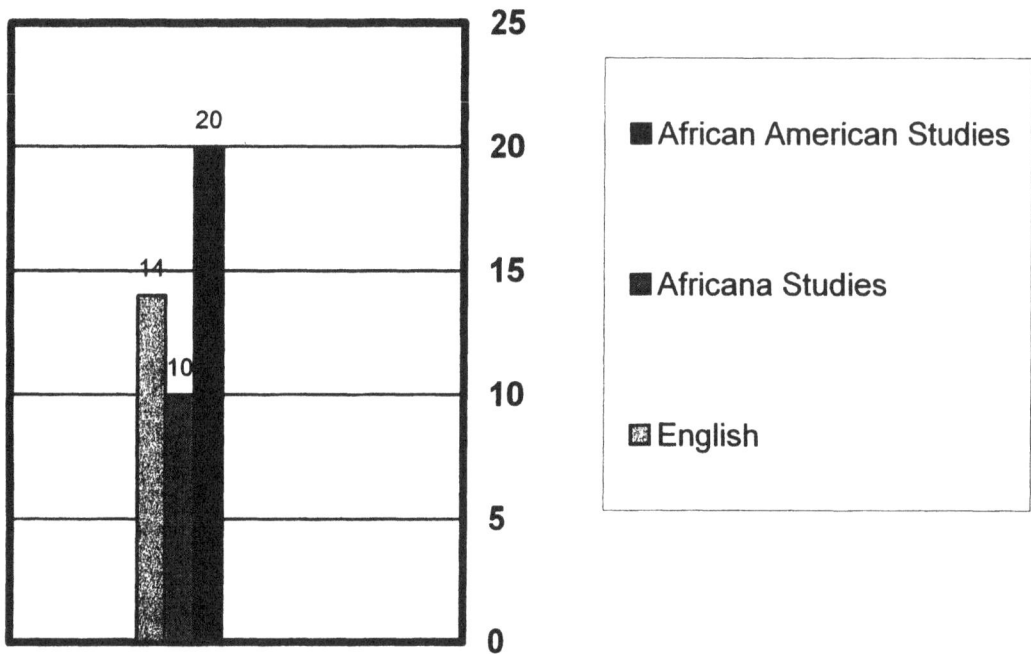

Legend:
- ■ African American Studies
- ■ Africana Studies
- ▦ English

Bar values: 20, 14, 10

APPENDIX F - Class Size

Survey Question 13: *What is the total number of students enrolled in the AAS courses you recently taught?*

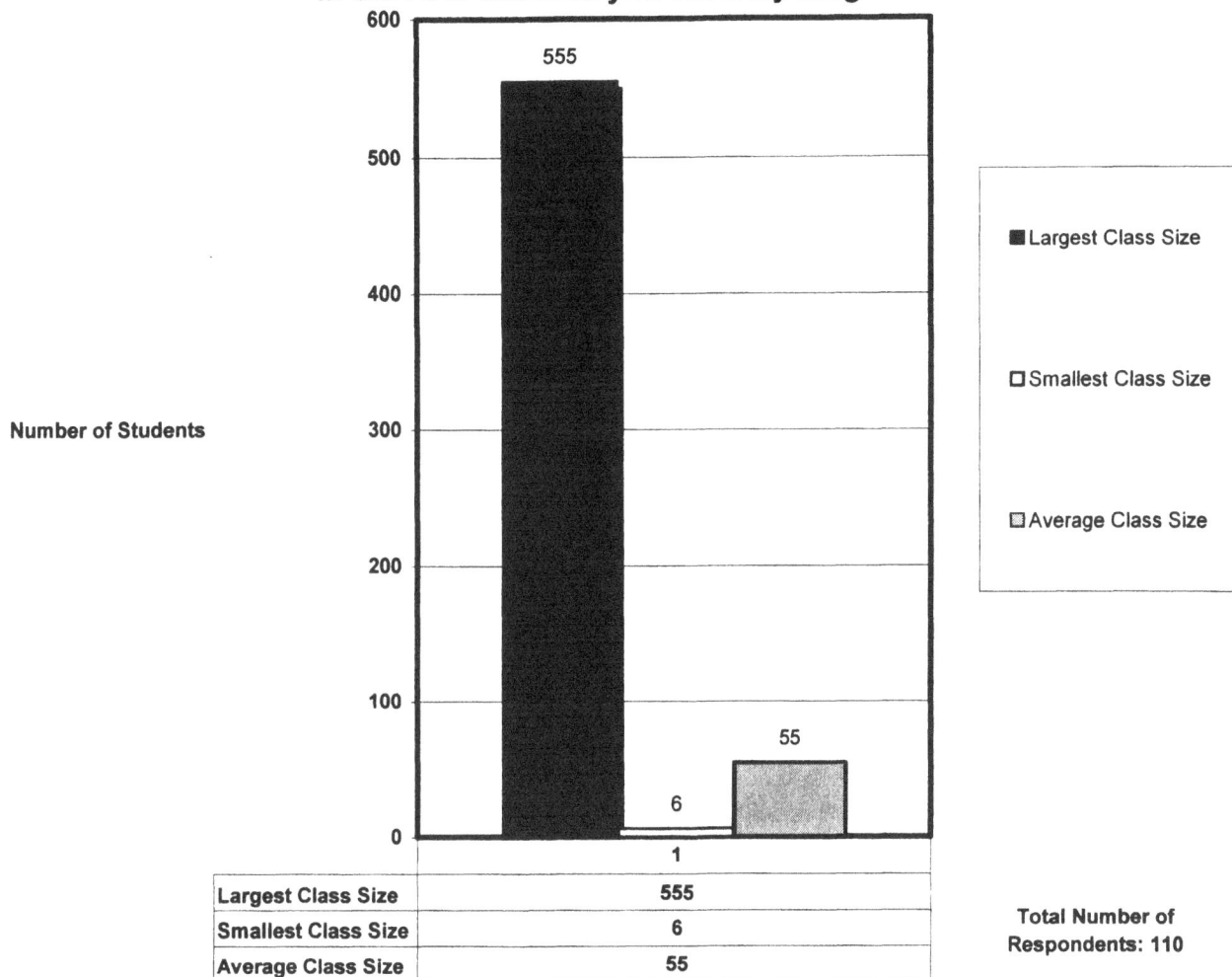

Number of Students

Legend:
- ■ Largest Class Size
- □ Smallest Class Size
- ▨ Average Class Size

Largest Class Size	555
Smallest Class Size	6
Average Class Size	55

Total Number of Respondents: 110

APPENDIX G - Difficulty Finding Materials

Survey Question 14: *Do you find it difficult to secure books and other instructional resources in AAS in your library or campus bookstore?*

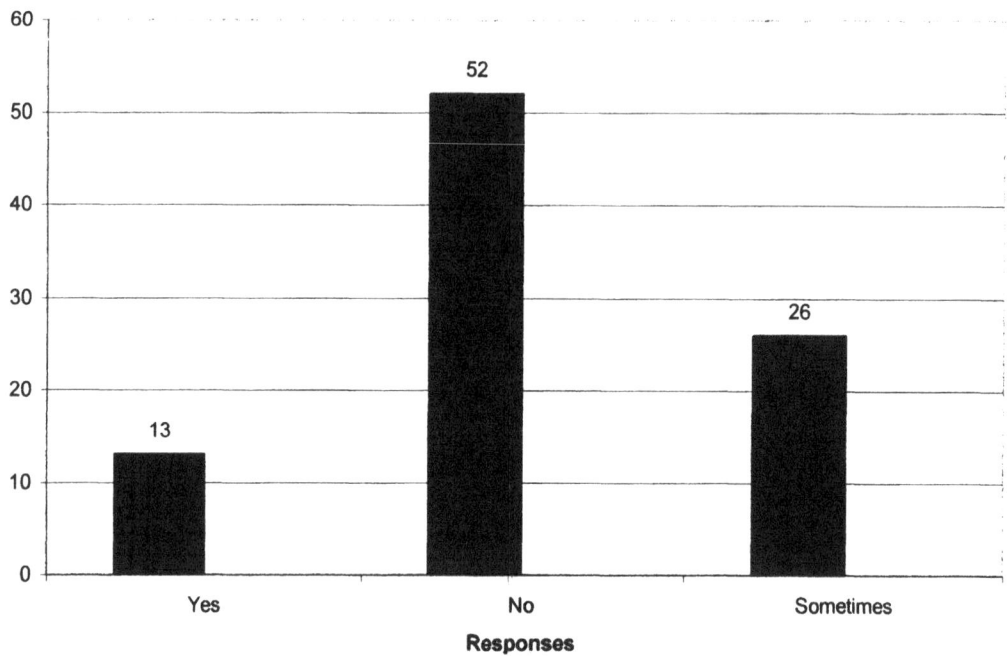

Total Number of Respondents: 91

APPENDIX H - Questions 14 –18 Survey Responses

Questions 14 through 18 focus on the ability of faculty to locate materials within their institution's library collection. The purpose is to find out if the faculty thinks that the library satisfies the needs of African-American scholars and students.

Question 14.

Do you find it difficult to secure books and other instructional resources in AAS in your library or campus bookstore?

107 Total Respondents

39 Yes　　　　　**37 No**　　　　　**31 Sometimes**

Question 15.

If you marked "yes" or "sometimes," please check all the reasons that apply:

___Out of print　　　　　___Too expensive　　　　　___Not in Library

___Not enough copies in Library　　　___Not readily available, because…

88 Total Respondents

<u>29</u> **Out of print**　　　<u>11</u> **Too expensive**

<u>25</u> **Not in Library**　　<u>11</u> **Not enough copies**

<u>12</u> **not readily available, because…**

- "They were lost or stolen." (cited 4 or more times)
- "Many are damaged and cannot be replaced."
- "Difficult to locate small publishers or reliable suppliers."
- "Little interest in developing Black studies."
- "Subject resources not available."
- "Very little funding for books in this area."
- "Lack of knowledge about Black resources."
- "No interest."
- "Not subscribed to."

Question 16.

List the subject areas in which you find it difficult to locate appropriate books and other instructional resources:

85 Total Respondents to question

Subject Areas listed by respondents:

Basic Introductory texts	Afro-Am primary sources	Afro-Latin studies
Contemporary Africa	Black Art/Artists	African Philosophy
Afro-Am Economic studies	Current works on Black Family	Black Psychology
18th/19th century Literature	Black Male/Female Issues	Ancient Africa
Modern Black Writers	Folklore & Storytelling	Black Music
Black studies Criticism	Black Political Theory	Black in Films
African Leadership	Basic Surveys	Cape Verdean studies
Caribbean studies	Kemetic studies	Child studies
Multicultural Psychology	African Novels	African Cinema

African Centered Education Paradigms

Contemporary books and films on African-American studies and the African Diaspora

Question 17.

How frequently do you electronically access or physically use your institution's library to prepare for instruction of AAS courses?

107 Total Respondents to question 17

54 Frequently	**32 Occasionally**	**17 Rarely**	**3 Never**

Question 18.

Do You find that your institution's library has the majority of items needed for instruction in African-American studies?

___Yes   ___No   Comment (optional):

83 Total Respondents to question 18

72 Yes   21 No

Selected Comments:

- "The library made a commitment over 25 years ago to build a strong Africana collection."
- "It can be difficult sometimes, I have relied upon my personal library."
- "I purchase want I need and place it on reserve."
- "I take charge of my situation and have learned not to depend upon the library."
- It makes a great difference to have a Black studies librarian who is extremely alert, vigilant, highly competent and regarded."
- "Library notifies me when it receives materials in my research area."
- "We are lucky to belong to a consortium of Ohio colleges; I can get materials from any of them."
- "Range has greatly expanded through institutional cooperation."
- "Library needs more subscriptions to Black journals"
- "Need scholarly journals focused on African-American affairs."
- "African-American journals and magazines are a problem area."
- "Fortunate to have an excellent library for teaching and research purposes."
- "Fortunate to have an independent bookstore near the campus."
- "I have worked with the library to increase holdings in all AAS areas."
- "Very weak in Black music holdings, scores, CD, tapes, etc."
- "No known texts on the subject of 'Race and Criminal Justice.'"
- "Desired subject matter not treated in available text."
- "Need a basic survey text, students cannot afford multiple books that analyzes time periods, i.e. 'the sixties.'"
- "Most materials are from 1960s-1980, slow to acquire new materials."
- "High percentage of Black studies materials are stolen or lost."
- "Have asked publishers directly for materials, but no reply."
- "Our Black Cultural Center has a library."
- "Need new books on contemporary African society."
- "More films and videotapes."
- "This is a difficult question to answer accurately."
- "Yes, I ordered them!"
- "But, there is always room for improvement."

APPENDIX I - Survey Respondents by Department

All 124 returned faculty survey forms are numbered here and listed by the <u>Administrative Department Home</u> and <u>Subject or Course Taught</u>. Unique course titles were selected to illustrate variety of courses and subjects taught. Multiple courses and subjects are noted as "Thematic." Senior and graduate level courses are noted by the term "Seminars."

<u>Department Home</u>	<u>Subject/Course Taught</u>
1. History	Comparative Slave Systems
2. English	AA Literature/Thematic
3. African-American studies	History-Regional (Latin Am.)
4. Educational Policy studies	Education of Blacks in the U.S.
5. Psychiatry	African-American Identity
6. Afro-American studies	Philosophy/History/Literature
7. Art	Visual Art & Sculpture
8. Communications	African Am. History - Thematic
9. Sociology	Race and Ethnicity
10. Sociology	Introduction to African-Am. studies
11. African-American studies	Psychology/Family studies
12. English	Comparative Literature/African Lit.
13. African-American studies	Music/Intro to African-Am studies
15. African-American studies	African History/Culture
14. Sociology	Black Communities/Family
16. English	Creative Writing
17. African studies	Anthropology
18. History	History - post 1865
19. Political Science	Intro/Black Politics/Comparative
20. Communication Arts	African-American Theatre
21. Music	African-American Music
22. English	Literature/Black Masculinity
23. English	African Am. Political Theory
24. Sociology	Religion/Ethnicity/Social Change
25. Sociology/Anthropology	Peoples of Africa/ Ethnicity
26. African-American studies	Religion/ Popular Culture
27. Social Work	Black Family/Church/Society
28. Psychology	AA Psychology/ Black Feminism
29. History	African-American History/Survey
30. English	African Am. Literature – Thematic
31. Anthropology	Peoples and Cultures of Africa
32. Black Africana studies	Black Popular Culture
33. English	Contemporary Black Fiction
34. African-American studies	Literature/African/Caribbean
35. Philosophy	African/Non-Western Traditions
36. History	Latin Am/Africa and Middle East
37. Political Science	Intro/Black Power Ideology
38. History	Thematic/AA Intellectual Tradition
39. Sociology	African-American Male
40. African-American studies	African Politics
41. English	African-American Literature/Women
42. Education	African-American Women/Family

43. African-American studies	History/Art & Theatre/Govt/Soc.
44. History	Religion/Historical Survey
45. Art	African-American Art & Artists
46. Africana studies	Caribbean Literature/Women Writers
47. Political Science	Intro/Comparative Urban Politics
48. Africana studies	Intro/Black Music/Women's studies
49. History	Intro/Modern Africa/Southern Africa
50. Psychology/Social Work	Black Child/Black Family studies
51. Africana studies	Afro-Hispanic Literature/Drama
52. Africana studies	Blacks in Films/Black West/Intro
53. History	Intro/Survey/Thematic Seminars
54. African/African-American studies	Democratic Theory/Afro-Brazil
55. Sociology	Race Relations/Minority Groups
56. Black studies	Intro to AAS/Thematic/Resistance
57. Health and Human Services	Black Health – not taught in 6-7 yrs.
58. English	African-American Literature
59. African-American studies	Psychology/Melanin Biology
60. Anthropology	Childhood: The African Experience
61. Anthropology	Peoples and Cultures of Africa
62. None provided	
63. None provided	
64. Black studies	Thematic/Black Nationalism
65. Anthropology/Geography	Thematic/North African Sex Roles
66. Political Science	Thematic/Civil Rights & Voting
67. Political Science	African Politics/African Am. Politics
68. African-American studies	Introduction to Black studies
69. African-American studies	African Politics/Pan-Africanism
70. African-American studies/Anthropology	Intro to AAS/Cultural Heritage
71. Sociology/Anthropology	The Rural South/Gullah Culture
72. Sociology/Anthropology	Caribbean Culture, Identity/Politics
73. History	Survey/Thematic/New Deal/ WWII
74. Sociology	Introduction/Criminal Justice
75. African-American studies	History/Intro to Afrocentricity
76. NO AAS program or department	-------
77. History	African-Americans Leadership
78. Sociology	Minorities & Criminal Justice
79. Modern Languages	Afro-Hispanic Literature
80. History	Civil Rights Movement
81. Afro-American studies	Survey/Health Care/Economics
82. Geography	African Geography
83. Afro-American studies	Literature/Harlem Renaissance
84. Africana studies	Law and Public Policy
85. School of Arts and Sciences	Comparative Race Relations
86. Africana studies	Intro to AAS/Thematic surveys
87. Have not taught AAS courses for several years.	
88. Music	Intro/African-American Music
89. Psychology	Classic studies Black Psychology
90. Ethnic studies	History/Thematic/Political Thought
91. African-American studies	AA Literature to the 1920s
92. Religious studies	AA Religious Experience
93. Minority studies	Black in Science and Technology
94. Music	Black women in Western Music
95. Sociology	Black Family/Public Policy/Law

96.	Africana studies	Free Blacks in Antebellum America
97.	History	Intro to AAS/Civil Rights Movement
98.	Africana studies	Survey of African America/Thematic
99.	Pan-African studies	Theatre & Drama/Thematic
100.	Ethnic studies	African-American Folklore
101.	English	African and the Diaspora
102.	African-American World studies	Intro/Literature/Thematic Seminars
103.	African-American studies	AA Women/AA Drama
104.	Pan-African studies	Multicultural Psych/Trad. Healing
105.	African-American studies/Sociology	AA and the Criminal Justice System
106.	Black studies	Intro to Black Politics/ Thematic
107.	Graduate College	Thematic Seminars
108.	NOT GIVEN	African-American Psychology
109.	Ethnomusicology	AA Musical Heritage/Seminars
110.	College of Arts and Sciences	AA Education/Intro/Seminars
111.	English	AA Literature/Thematic
112.	BAS-Black American studies	AA Community/Arts/Thematic
113.	History	African World/AA History/Thematic
114.	Ethnic studies	Black Social and Political Thought
115.	Anthropology	Black Cultural/Social Organization
116.	NOT GIVEN	Economics of African America
117.	Political Science	Black Political Participation in U.S.
118.	Drama	Intro/Contemporary AA Drama
119.	Social Work	Thematic/Ethnic Acculturation
120.	History	Thematic/Civil Rights Movement
121.	NONE	African-American Comedy
122.	African-American studies	Enslavement/Thematic
123.	Religious studies	AA Religions
124.	NOT GIVEN	African-American Male in Literature

TITLE INDEX

AUTHOR INDEX

www.ingramcontent.com/pod-product-compliance
Lightning Source LLC
Chambersburg PA
CBHW081157270326
41930CB00014B/3197